WORKING GUNDOGS
AND THEIR TRAINING

H. J. L. OSBOURN

Working Gundogs

AND THEIR TRAINING

COUNTRY LIFE BOOKS

DEDICATION

*With gratitude to my wife
who did not just stand and wait but
who has done much of that through many a
cold training session, working test,
field trial and shooting day from the
moors to the marshes.*

Published by Country Life Books
and distributed for them by
The Hamlyn Publishing Group Limited
London · New York · Sydney · Toronto
Astronaut House, Feltham, Middlesex, England

First published 1980
ISBN 0 600 31894 X

Set in 10 on 12 point Monophoto Plantin Light by
Tradespools Limited, Frome
Printed in England by
Hazell Watson & Viney Limited, Aylesbury

Contents

GUNDOG PUP

Make much of me,
Your gundog pup,
And when you think I'm growing up
Show me what I need to do
To be a complement to you.
Be patient with my learning
Which from my baby brain
May not be very fast.
Show me again
The hunting, stopping, turning,
And I will understand at last.

When you take me shooting
I may be tempted but will not chase,
Watch me close and guide me
To the pheasant's hiding place
And I will hunt and crash the brambles
Jump the fence and swim the stream
Pick up and scramble quickly back
To you the leader of my pack.

I will fulfil our dream.

H.J.L.O.

Foreword

Many thanks are due from the author to those who have helped him in the production of this book.

First I am grateful to Commander John Williams, Secretary of the Kennel Club, and to his Club, for permission to reproduce their standards which are so important in telling us how our dogs should look. I believe that it is proper that all gundog lovers should be quite sure that their dogs are of typical conformation so that breeds are preserved in good shape and are not bred too small or too big. Both these faults are apparent in most breeds today. Then I must thank Lulu Pelly and Joanna Osbourn for much labour over their typewriters and my appalling handwriting.

The photographers have contributed an important part of the book. Anne Roslin-Williams produced the entirely new and splendid colour photographs and she, John Tarleton and John Marchington the black and white photographs.

Introduction

This book is written as a guide to the man, or woman, thinking of getting a gundog to use for its proper purpose of finding or retrieving game – or of doing both. It should guide you towards the sort of dog to have and then tell you how to train it to do what it has been bred to do.

It is important that you buy a dog suited to the purpose you have in mind. Dogs have been bred over the centuries to do certain things superbly well if properly handled, and disappointment is bound to ensue if you buy a dog suited to one purpose and try to train it to perform another. If you want to wander around alone or with one companion, shooting rough and expecting a rabbit, a hare, a pigeon, a pheasant, a duck or a snipe to be pushed up within shooting distance, you want a spaniel. They hunt close country and tough cover and can be trained to remain no more than 30 or 40 yards from your gun whilst they go about their business of pushing game from its hiding place. If that is your sort of shooting don't buy a retriever. You can train a retriever to hunt, but it will not do it as efficiently or as energetically as a spaniel, and you will not be happy with the outcome. If your shooting is mostly of driven pheasants don't buy a spaniel, for it will be miserable sitting by your side at interminable drives. A spaniel will retrieve shot pheasants but not as well or as happily as a retriever, so again you will be unhappy at the outcome. If your shooting takes you to the uplands and moorlands where distances are vast and game scarce don't buy a spaniel or a retriever. They can be trained to hunt up grouse or quail, but they have not the scope or pace to cover the country quickly. They do not hold their heads high to pick up distant scent and point or set the game's position. For this work you want pointers or setters. They will also retrieve for you if you insist, but it is not their instinctive action, and a specialist retriever will do that part of the job better. But for big open country the pointer or setter is the dog to lead you to the game.

You might buy a pointer/retriever expecting it to encompass all the jobs of hunting, flushing, pointing and retrieving. Their protagonists insist that these breeds will do all these things. I do not altogether agree with these enthusiasts. I think pointer/retrievers do a spaniel's work very well, but not better than a spaniel. They do a retriever's work, but not better than a retriever, and they do not in my view have the scope or range to cover ground as extensively as a pointer or setter although they can certainly be trained to point. But a pointer/retriever is a good all-round dog capable of being a wonderful companion to the rough shooter. More than that should not, I think, be expected, but what they can do will produce endless pleasure.

So you must buy dogs for jobs. Then you must train them. This is a great thrill, but it cannot be done by anyone, and it cannot be done without much time and a lot of patience. It cannot be done by anyone lacking dog sense, patience, kindness, understanding and a very controllable temper. Plenty of people will never train a dog because they are unsuited to the task, and only self-criticism and hopeless results will prove the trainer's unsuitability. Many people on the other hand have it in them to start from scratch and train their first dog. Regular tuition of short duration is required, not irregular and prolonged lessons. Little by little is the method.

If you use this book as a guide to the right dog and follow the training instructions carefully you could be a great success. On the other hand you could make a complete mess of the job. Take heart. Even experts get things wrong and have to go back to the beginning. It is easy to see why. Dogs vary in temperament and intelligence just as do human beings. There are precocious dogs quick to learn and late developers slow to understand. Your expertise must include the ability to recognise the type of dog on which you are working and set the pace of the instruction accordingly. That is a difficult thing to do and separates the great from the ordinary trainer.

Training a gundog is always a roller-coaster affair – soaring to great heights of elation and plumbing terrible depths of despair. Do remember that this is normal. When things go wrong, give long thought as to the reason. It is almost certainly your fault and, recognising this, you must go back to the stage you had reached before things went wrong and start slowly to build again. I assure you that, given decent material, you will return to success. If you could hear of my disasters you would take heart and try again to build the perfect dog. Of course the instinct must be there. If you choose a dog with years of show bench breeding, no genius of yours will convert that animal into a skilled hunting dog. Those instincts will long ago have been bred out of it. But if you buy a dog from good field trial and shooting stock the basic instinct to hunt or retrieve will be firmly instilled and needs only your careful nurturing to bring it bursting into use.

Remember always that all dogs, including well-bred gundogs, have the instinct to chase. That is a primeval hound instinct. A gundog must not chase. Your main task is to convert that instinct to chase into a reflex to stop. Until your dog will stop instantly to the flush of fur or feather or the fall of game after a shot it is quite useless as a gundog. When it will stop instantly you are on the way. It has been truly said that 'a dog you can stop is a made dog'. Your task is to instil this stopping reflex very firmly whilst not inhibiting the dog's desire to hunt or retrieve. It is keeping this delicate balance between the firm discipline of stopping and the free-flowing expression of hunting, swimming and retrieving that is the trainer's constant problem.

I hope this book helps you to keep the balance and reap the immense rewards of handling a well-trained dog of your choice.

CHAPTER ONE

The Natural History of the Gundog

There was for many years a scientific debate about the ancestry of the domestic dog. Some experts held that there was such a variety of dogs, from the huge mastiff to the tiny chihuahua, that their ancestors must have been differing archetypes. Others thought that the domestication of the dog had started with the taming, by early man, of pack-hunting wolves. The latest acceptable research supports this latter theory, and it is now established by Fiennes that the domestic dog, all types of which are classed as *Canis familiaris*, is descended from four groups of wild wolves which are classed as *Canis lupus*. These four groups are the Dingo Group derived from the pale-footed Asian wolf (*Canis lupus pallipes*); the Northern Group derived mainly from the Northern wolf (*Canis lupus*); the Greyhound Group derived from a cursorial wolf ancestor related to *Canis lupus pallipes*; and the Mastiff Group derived from mountain wolves such as the Tibetan wolf (*Canis lupo chanco* or laniger). It is from this last group that today's gundogs, such as spaniels, pointers, setters and retrievers, are descended as are modern mastiffs, Newfoundlands and bulldogs.

We know that dog and man existed together long ago from archaeological research, ancient cave paintings and decorations to the tombs of Egyptian Pharaohs and Chinese Emperors. Dogs' bones disinterred from alongside those of men in Scandinavia show that they co-existed 10,000 years ago, and even earlier indications come from cave paintings in Altamira and Lascaux which date back to 15,000–10,000 BC.

By Neolithic times (5,000–2,000 BC) man had started to use stone axes to fell trees and to hollow out canoes, and he had become a settler instead of a nomad. Excavations show that at that time dogs had been part of man's domestic scene along with the longer-domesticated cattle, sheep and goats. Man had almost certainly shared a hunting relationship with packs of dogs when they both were itinerant hunters. The advantages were mutual, for dogs could kill and man could take the carcass, or man could snare and the dog could scavenge on the remains.

Man became more an agriculturalist as the ice of the last Ice Age receded, and he began to use dogs for herding and guarding. It was not a problem to domesticate the dog because they have very strongly developed tribal and territorial instincts which give rise to the existence of the herd with a pack leader. Thus a whelp brought from the nest to the cave for upbringing would transfer its allegiance to its human dictator and become tame and tractable. From this man–dog relationship and from the four main groups many types of dog were produced in many parts of the world as gods, as playthings, for guarding, for shepherding and for hunting, but those descended from the mastiff group are of interest to the study of gundogs.

Compared with the advent of civilisation in the Far and Middle East the Neolithic revolution came late to the people of Europe. When it came a major trade route, known as the great amber route, was developed along the Rhine and the Danube to take amber and other northern products down to the Mediterranean for trading with the products of the East. Into these Mediterranean countries from the Middle East came sight-hunting greyhounds evolved in wide deserts for chasing deer and hare, while spreading westwards from the highlands of Tibet came the mastiffs descended from the Tibetan wolf (*Canis lupus chanco*). From this breed came the main canine populations of Classical times, much prized in war and hunting and as guards for homesteads and flocks, and important enough to be carved in bas relief on tombs and monuments. These dogs came out of the mountains stretching almost unbroken from Tibet to Europe through the Anatolian mountains, the Alps, the Massif Central of France and the Pyrenees. Typical of the big dogs of these high lands were today's Pyrenean mountain dogs, Great Danes, Newfoundland and bloodhound types like the St Bernard, and from them were evolved today's gundogs. The Pyrenean mountain dog, descended from Molossian mastiffs, is the ancestor of the land spaniels, an important link in the gundog chain. What these dogs had in common were an acute power of scent, the possession of an acute stop on the muzzle, which was relatively short, large floppy ears and fine silky coats. These true scent-hunting hounds have evolved to produce dogs varying in size from the bloodhound to the dachshund and to embrace dogs of the pointer type, spaniels, setters and retrievers.

The first domesticated use of mastiff types was probably that of a guard dog for sheep in its mountain home. They earned a reputation for fierceness and courage and were used in large numbers in war as an attacking force and for hunting large animals such as lions, elephants and horses. We know that the tribe of the Molossi of Epirus owned these fierce shepherd dogs for war, as did the Hyrcanian peoples who lived in Baluchistan and northern India. These two main mastiff lines came together in ancient Greece, so that Molossian and Hyrcanian hounds came to share a common ancestry as they flowed through into Europe. These dogs came to Britain with the invasions of the Angles and Saxons who, since they were Germanic peoples, probably introduced a line related to the German boarhounds and the Great Dane.

From this stock man's ingenuity in breeding dogs especially for hunting up and recovering game has produced gundogs of great variety.

The earliest use of dogs for the pursuit of game entailed the use of their pack-hunting instinct to drive animals towards hidden pits or slingers or bowmen. Later the prey was driven into nets, and birds were flushed to the bow or to be stooped to by falcons and hawks and finally to be shot by the fowlingpiece. In open country were developed gaze-hounds such as greyhounds, salukis and borzois to chase game across plains, and in close country the dog's pack instinct led to the hunting of stag and boar with packs of hounds.

Whilst the evolution of these large dogs was in progress, their size dictated by the size of their prey and the openness of their habitat, in southern Europe and Spain there grew a demand for small dogs to push birds from cover – the spaniel – or larger ones to find hidden game – the pointer. Here is the genesis of the gundog. These breeds grew out of stock which came from India, and one of their distinct features is their multiple markings with flecks and spots on coats of different colours, a quality seen today in pointers, spaniels, setters and sheepdogs. The pointer-type is almost certainly ancestral to the true spaniels such as the Old English Water Dogge and the Breton spaniel. Britain and Brittany were covered in lowland forest, boggy and marshy, and it was this type of country which dictated the spaniel type of dog as the most desirable, for they could shoulder their way through the undergrowth to push out game. In Romano-British times both springer- and cocker-type spaniels were being bred, though they were only the big and small type of one breed. The bigger one was used to hunt up and 'spring' game and the smaller to start small game such as woodcock – the early beginnings of springers and cockers.

The hunting of birds with hound and hawk continued through medieval times. It was the advent of the muzzle-loading shotgun which demanded the production of the pointer to range wide and to locate and hold game. They were to hand as a basic type and needed merely training to teach them to creep forward silently and lead the gunner to the hidden game. Once the game was located they stood at 'point', indicating by the attitude of their body and outstretched muzzle the precise location. Game and dog froze in this cataleptic pose until the gunner arrived to push the dog forward so as to flush the game and thus to give the hunter a chance to shoot with his single-shot gun. The pointers were very slow and deliberate, which suited their masters, whose shooting, with a five minute reloading time, was slow and deliberate too.

As guns became faster, with the breach-loader, a faster dog was demanded, and from big spaniel stock was bred the long-legged setter. These dogs located game and sat down or 'set' to its whereabouts until moved forward to flush, and they had the speed to match the newer weapons.

In the eighteenth and nineteenth centuries new riches and open farmland produced the sport of walking up partridges and driving pheasants, grouse and partridges over stationary guns. The *battue*, which grew to grotesque proportions with thousands of birds being killed in a day, brought with it the need for specialist retrievers. The first was the flatcoat bred from the Newfoundland and St John's dog or Labrador, but by the late nineteenth century the Labrador, which despite being much used for interbreeding retained its type, had swept all before it as the ideal retriever.

Around this time sportsmen in Central Europe were evolving dogs which they wished to hunt, point and retrieve – the all-purpose gundog, in fact, that would contain in itself the abilities of the pointer, the spaniel and the retriever. They took the pointer from England, where it had been perfected from its big, slow Spanish forebear, mixed it with French hound blood and the genes of their own hunting dogs and evolved the Weimaraner, the German short-haired pointer and the Viszla.

So it remains today. Springers are strong, cockers exist but poorly, the golden retriever and the flatcoat limp in the wake of the Labrador, and all-purpose gundogs developed as specialists from the English pointer are growing as breeds which 'hunt, point and retrieve' – all the sportsman's requirements rolled into one.

CHAPTER TWO

Spaniels

The job of spaniels is to be hunting and flushing dogs. Their speciality is to shoulder their way through cover, however impenetrable to search out and to locate game. Their instinct is to investigate every corner of the country to be shot whether there is game present or not.

They should be trained to hunt a gunshot away from the shooter because their habit is to push up game from its seat as soon as it is located. Their docked stems work furiously as they hunt, and their energy is seemingly inexhaustible. They should sit to flush and wait until told to retrieve. Retrieving is not their best accomplishment, but they are very successfully trained to it. They are good in water and much in demand as the wildfowler's dog on the marsh. They are used as beaters in the line on days of driven game – a function they fulfil to perfection.

For a one-man dog they are, in the shape of the springer spaniel, without equal.

Spaniels are the oldest of the gundogs. They were in Britain doing their hunting job in AD 150. We know this because the Roman poet Oppian wrote at that time about the 'wild tribes of Britons' and said they had 'a valiant breed of tracking dog by the name Agasseus', asserting that 'with its nose especially the Agassian dog is most excellent, and for tracking it is the best of all.' We shall never know for how long this British dog had had these hunting skills, but 18 centuries is a long time for the spaniel to be in existence and certainly longer than any other gundog.

Nearly all the spaniels have had their moments of popularity, but now the springer is the only really superb performer. Cockers are hanging on by a toenail, the field spaniel is practically extinct as is the clumber. The Irish water spaniel has a few enthusiastic adherents, but the Welsh, which may be the original Agassian dog, and the Brittany, its near cousin, which not only hunts but points, are the subjects of considerable activity in France and America.

SPRINGER SPANIEL

The Kennel Club Standard says, 'The English springer is the oldest of our sporting gundogs and the taproot from which all of our sporting land spaniels (clumbers excepted) have been evolved. It was originally used for the purpose of finding and springing game for the net, falcon or greyhound . . . The breed is of ancient and pure origin, and should be kept as such.'

There is no doubt that spaniels are an ancient race of dog as archaeological finds and prehistoric wall paintings indicate. They were probably indigenous to Great Britain at the dawn of Christianity, for writings by the Roman poet Strabo of around the year 1 BC and by Oppian of AD 200 both mention the existence of dogs which the Britons used for hunting their swampy and afforested country and which according to Strabo were important enough to be mentioned as being exported alongside cattle, gold, silver and slaves. Oppian calls this British dog the Agassian Dog, and excavation of a Roman villa at the village of Hinton St Mary in Dorset has revealed floor tiles with a picture of a spaniel-type dog hunting up a stag. Hywel Dda (Howell the Good), King of Wales between AD 918 and 950, produced enlightened laws which embraced the keeping and hunting of dogs including spaniels, and the Bayeux Tapestry illustrating William the Conqueror's triumph over Harold of England was embroidered in 1092 and shows the kings with dogs hunting for the hawk as spaniels customarily did.

The earliest recorded use of the word 'spaniel' in English literature is in 1387 in a poem by Chaucer. The name comes from the French '*espaignol*', which means Spanish, so it is believed that it originated in Spain, a descendant of the Pyrenean mountain dog.

From 1500 there is considerable literary reference to the existence of spaniels, the most famous of which was written in 1550 by Dr Johannes Caius and called *Of Englishe Dogges, the Diversities, the Names, the Nature and the Properties.* He identified land spaniel, setter and water spaniel as dogs which 'Sought the bird and showed its flight by pursuit'. He described the land spaniel thus: 'For most part their skins are white and if they be marked with any spots they are commonly red and somewhat great therewithall . . . Otherwise of them be reddish and blackish, but of that sort there be but very few. There is also at this day among us a new kind of dog brought out of France and they are speckled all over with white and black which mingled colours incline to a marble blue.' Today the Kennel Club says they 'should preferably be liver and white, black and

Springer spaniel negotiating a fence with a woodcock

A spaniel brings in a pigeon under briar and barb

white or either of those colours with tan markings'. Springers do not change with the passing of centuries. Today the springer is the outstanding gundog, equipped to hunt and retrieve in almost any conditions and strong enough to crash through apparently impenetrable cover or swim against a rip-tide carrying a goose. Centuries of work flow in its blood.

Spaniel (English Springer)

CHARACTERISTICS The English springer is the oldest of our sporting gundogs and the taproot from which all of our sporting land spaniels (clumbers excepted) have been evolved. It was originally used for the purpose of finding and springing game for the net, falcon or greyhound, but at the present time it is used entirely to find, flush and retrieve game for the gun. The breed is of ancient and pure origin, and should be kept as such.

GENERAL APPEARANCE The general appearance of the modern springer is that of a symmetrical, compact, strong, upstanding, merry and active dog, built for endurance and activity. He is the highest on the leg and raciest in build of all British land spaniels.

HEAD AND SKULL The skull should be of medium length and fairly broad and slightly rounded, rising from the foreface, making a brow or stop, divided by a fluting between the eyes gradually dying away along the forehead towards the occiput bone, which should not be peaked. The cheeks should be flat, that is not rounded or full. The foreface should be of proportionate length to the skull, fairly broad and deep without being coarse, well chiselled below the eyes, fairly deep and square in flew, but not exaggerated to such an extent as would interfere with comfort when retrieving. Nostrils well developed.

EYES The eyes should be neither too full nor too small but of medium size, not prominent nor sunken but well set in (not showing haw) of an alert, kind expression. A mouse-like eye without expression is objectionable, as also is a light eye. The colour should be dark hazel.

EARS The ears should be lobular in shape, set close to the head, of good length and width, but not exaggerated. The correct set should be in line with the eye.

MOUTH The jaws should be strong, with a perfect regular and complete scissor bite, i.e., the upper teeth closely overlapping the lower teeth and set square to the jaws.

NECK The neck should be strong and muscular, of nice length and free from throatiness, well set in the shoulders, nicely arched and tapering towards the head – thus giving great activity and speed. A ewe neck is objectionable.

FOREQUARTERS The forelegs should be straight and nicely feathered, elbows set well to body and with proportionate substance to carry the body, strong flexible pasterns.

BODY The body should be strong and of proportionate length, neither too long nor too short, the chest deep and well developed with plenty of heart and lung room, well-sprung ribs, loin muscular and strong with slight arch, and well coupled, thighs broad and muscular and well developed.

HINDQUARTERS The hindlegs should be well let down from hip to hocks. Stifles and hocks moderately bent, inclining neither inwards nor outwards. Coarseness of hocks objectionable.

FEET Feet tight, compact and well rounded with strong full pads.

GAIT The springer's gait is strictly his own. His forelegs should swing straight forward from the shoulder, throwing the feet well forward in an easy and free manner. His hocks should drive well under his body, following in a line with the forelegs. At slow movements many springers have a pacing stride typical of the breed.

TAIL The stern should be low and never carried above the level of the back, well feathered and with a lively action.

COAT The coat should be close, straight and weather resisting without being coarse.

COLOUR Any recognised land spaniel colour is acceptable, but liver and white, black and white, or either of these colours with tan markings preferred.

WEIGHT AND SIZE The approxinate height should be 51 cm (20 in). The approximate weight should be 22·7 kg (50 lb).

NOTE Male animals should have two apparently normal testicles fully descended into the scrotum.

WELSH SPRINGER SPANIEL

The Welsh springer spaniel comes between the English springer and the cocker in size. It should always breed true to its distinctive colours of white and red. Protagonists of the Welsh assert that it is a breed separate from all other spaniels because of its distinctive coat and its ears which are small, pointed and vineleaf-shaped instead of being heavy and pendulous as in other spaniels. Writing in 1550 Dr Johannes Caius in his treatise *Of Englishe Dogges* identified the land spaniel and said: 'The most part their skins are white and if they be marked with any spots they are commonly red, and somewhat great therewithall.' There is the evidence of a red and white dog on a floor mosaic unearthed from a Roman villa at Hinton St Mary in North Dorset, dated AD 300, and there is also reference to white and red hunting dogs in Welsh literature of the twelfth century.

Whatever their antiquity the Welsh, known in Wales as 'starters' rather than springers, were recognised by the Kennel Club only in 1902. This was largely through the efforts of a Mr A. T. Williams whose family has bred them without outcross for over 100 years. In 1895 he got a dog called Flint from the then famous Llanharan Kennels. Williams registered Flint at the Kennel Club as Corrin and, as the Welsh was not then recognised by the Kennel Club, Corrin was registered as a cocker, in which guise he was unbeatable at shows. When the Welsh breed was recognised Corrin was registered as a Welsh springer spaniel and continued to win under his new classification until he was 10 years old. Corrin was a heavy dog weighing 47 lb, but nevertheless he sired many fine Welsh which formed the backbone of the breed. From 1925 a bitch called Goitre Lass was mated frequently with a dog Ch. Merglan Bang, and it is probable that all modern Welsh have blood from this mating in their veins.

The Welsh is a strong active dog bred to hunt up Welsh mountains, but it has failed to reach the popularity of the English springer or the cocker and is nowadays rarely seen in field trials, perhaps because they need great care in training and have a strong predisposition to hunt a line forward instead of quartering. It is such a good-looking dog and of such antiquity that it is a shame to see it falling into desuetude, although enthusiasts in Wales, America and Holland keep the breed alive if not working.

Spaniel (Welsh Springer)

CHARACTERISTICS The 'Welsh spaniel' or 'springer' is also known and referred to in Wales as a 'starter'. He is of very ancient and pure origin, and is a distinct variety.

GENERAL APPEARANCE A symmetrical, compact, strong, merry, very active dog; not stilty; obviously built for endurance and hard work. A quick and active mover displaying plenty of push and drive.

HEAD AND SKULL Skull proportionate, of moderate length, slightly domed, with clearly defined stop and well chiselled below the eyes. Muzzle of medium length, straight, fairly square; the nostrils well developed and flesh-coloured or dark. A short chubby head is objectionable.

EYES Hazel or dark, medium size, not prominent, nor sunken, nor showing haw.

EARS Set moderately low and hanging close to the cheeks, comparatively small and gradually narrowing towards the tip and shaped somewhat like a vineleaf, covered with setter-like feathering.

MOUTH The jaws should be strong, with a perfect regular and complete scissor bite, i.e., the upper teeth closely overlapping the lower teeth and set square to the jaws.

NECK Long and muscular, clean in throat, neatly set into long sloping shoulders.

FOREQUARTERS Forelegs of medium length, straight, well boned, moderately feathered.

BODY Not long; strong and muscular with deep brisket, well-sprung ribs; length of body should be proportionate to length of leg, and very well balanced; muscular loin slightly arched and well coupled up.

HINDQUARTERS Strong and muscular, wide and fully developed with deep second thighs. Hind legs well boned, hocks well let down; stifles moderately bent (neither turned in nor out), moderately feathered.

English springer spaniel: F.T. Ch. Crowhill Raffle

Welsh springer spaniel: Athelwood Uncle Sam

Cocker spaniel: Jungle of Mansergh

Clumber spaniel: Maladetta Tallman

Sussex spaniel: Novacroft Hello Holly

Field spaniel: Ch. Adam of Elmbury

FEET Round, with thick pads. Firm and cat-like, not too large or spreading.

TAIL Well set on and low, never carried above the level of the back; lightly feathered and lively in action.

COAT Straight or flat, of a nice silky texture, never wiry nor wavy. A curly coat is most objectionable.

COLOUR Rich red and white only.

WEIGHT AND SIZE A dog not to exceed 48 cm (19 in) in height at shoulder and a bitch 46 cm (18 in) approximately.

FAULTS Any departure from the foregoing points should be considered a fault, and the seriousness of the fault should be in exact proportion to its degree.

NOTE Male animals should have two apparently normal testicles fully descended into the scrotum.

COCKER SPANIEL

There is no doubt how the cocker got his name, for it comes from the task for which it was trained: to push up woodcock. It is a 'woodcocker'. It comes from the same stock as the springer, being bred from small dogs selected from litters. 'Stonehenge' in *The Dog* in 1879 says they were bred 'from the Sussex and old fashioned cocker of Devon or Wales selecting the blacks, so as now to become almost invariably of that colour'. The Sussex is golden liver in colour and so were the old fashioned Devon and Welsh cockers. The Kennel Club standard gives today's colour as 'various'. This is an indication of the great variety which has emerged from the original self colour of liver or black so that today they come in tones of blue, orange and chocolate as well as particolour and tricolours.

At the end of the nineteenth century, at dog shows, spaniel classes were divided by weight over and under 25 lb with litter brothers in both classes; but in 1901 the Spaniel Club abolished these limits, and cockers flourished as a separate breed. The breed was in important hands in the late 1800s, the most influential of which were those of Mr J. J. Farrow who in 1879 got a puppy which was destined to become Ch. Obo, a taproot of the breed. Another great cocker man, H. S. Lloyd, wrote in 1924 in *The Popular Cocker Spaniel*: 'Obo, it goes without saying, was the greatest force in the revival of the cocker, especially in the matter of size, for he and his progeny enabled breeders to utilize field spaniels (springers, as they were then termed) in the certainty that among the offspring there would be many small puppies ideal in size to the cocker breeder.'

A spaniel brings in a teal and shows its disdain for severe weather

Alas! the cocker became immensely popular as a pet in the 1930s, and its value as a gundog fell into decline. Now, according to the great expert Kieth Erlandson, it is hanging on by the tip of its paws in the field trial world and is much in need of the sponsorship of rich patrons to bring it back to the forefront today.

Spaniel (Cocker)

GENERAL APPEARANCE That of a merry sturdy sporting dog. The cocker spaniel should be well balanced and compact and should measure about the same from the withers to the ground as from the withers to the root of the tail.

HEAD AND SKULL There should be a good square muzzle with a distinct stop which should be mid way between the tip of the nose and the occiput. The skull should be well developed, cleanly chiselled, neither too fine nor too coarse. The cheek bones should not be prominent. The nose should be sufficiently wide to allow for the acute scenting power of this breed.

EYES The eyes should be full but not prominent, brown or dark brown in colour but never light, with a general expression of intelligence and gentleness though decidedly wide-awake, bright and merry. The rims should be tight.

EARS Lobular, set on low, on a level with the eyes, with fine feathers which extend to but not beyond the tip of the nose; well clothed with long silky hair which should be straight.

MOUTH Jaws should be strong and teeth should have a scissor bite.

NECK Neck should be moderate in length, clean in throat, muscular and neatly set in fine sloping shoulders.

FOREQUARTERS The shoulders should be sloping and fine, the chest well developed and the brisket deep, neither too wide nor too narrow in front. The legs must be well boned, feathered and straight and should be sufficiently short for concentrated power but not too short to interfere with the tremendous exertions expected from this grand little sporting dog.

BODY Body should be immensely strong and compact for the size and weight of the dog. The ribs should be well sprung behind the shoulder blades, the loin short, wide and strong, with a firm topline gently sloping downwards to the tail.

HINDQUARTERS Hindquarters should be wide, well rounded and very muscular. The legs must be well boned, feathered above the hock, with a good bend of stifle, and short below the hock allowing for plenty of drive.

FEET Feet should be firm, thickly padded and catlike.

TAIL Tail should be set on slightly lower than the line of the back; it must be merry, carried in line with the back and never cocked up. The tail should not be docked too long nor too short to interfere with its merry action.

COAT Flat and silky in texture, never wiry or wavy, with sufficient feather; not too profuse and never curly.

COLOUR Various. In self colours no white is allowed except on the chest.

GAIT There should be true through action both fore and aft, with great drive covering the ground well.

WEIGHT AND SIZE The weight should be about 12·7 to 14·5 kg (28–32 lb). The height at the withers should be approximately 38–39 cm (15–15½ in) for bitches and approximately 39–41 cm (15½–16 in) for dogs.

FAULTS Light bone; straight shoulder; flat ribs; unsound movement; weak hocks; weak pasterns; open or large feet; frown; small beady eyes; undershot or overshot mouth; uncertain or aggressive temperament.

NOTE Male animals should have two apparently normal testicles fully descended into the scrotum.

CLUMBER SPANIEL

The clumber is a heavy, massive dog which weighs twice as much as a cocker and 50 per cent more than a springer. Its head is big and, quite unlike those of other spaniels, square with heavy brows and muzzle. He hunts slowly and methodically but with great tenacity.

His origins are mysterious. We know that he took his English name from Clumber Park, the seat of the second Duke of Newcastle, who got a pack as a present from the French Duc de Noailles around the end of the eighteenth century. What we do not know is how they were produced, for no other similar dogs existed or exist in France. It may be that the Duc produced an absolutely unique dog on his estate and kept it entirely to himself, but if so it is a most unusual occurrence. It can be conjectured that the clumber is a cross between a French bassett and old English spaniel and maybe the great head and the haw of the eye comes from the bassett or the bloodhound. In any event there were none in England until the Duke of Newcastle got his original stock and none remaining in France after the Duc de Noailles gave his kennel away. The clumber was very successful in early field trials between 1899 and 1905, and they were much used in teams beating slowly but surely through thick cover. In 1925 King George V gave the breed a fillip when he re-established them at Sandringham, where teams pushed through the thick rhododendrons there which were practically impenetrable to beaters and too full of game for other spaniels to show the slow hunting steadiness of the clumber. Nowadays the clumber is practically unknown in the shooting field, having given way to the surge of the English springer.

Spaniel (Clumber)

GENERAL APPEARANCE That of a dog with a thoughtful expression, very massive but active, which moves with a rolling gait characteristic of the breed.

HEAD AND SKULL Head large, square and massive, of medium length, broad on top, with a decided occiput; heavy brows with a deep stop; heavy muzzle, with well-developed flew, and level jaw and mouth. Nose square and flesh-coloured.

EYES Dark amber, slightly sunk with some haw showing.

EARS Large, vineleaf-shaped, and well covered with straight hair, and hanging slightly forward, the feather not to extend below the leather.

MOUTH Should be level and neither over- nor undershot.

NECK Fairly long, thick and powerful, and well feathered underneath.

The almost extinct clumber spaniel displays his fine broad head over a hen pheasant

FOREQUARTERS Shoulders strong, sloping and muscular; chest deep. Legs short, straight, thick and strong.

BODY Long and heavy, and near the ground, with well-sprung ribs. Back straight, broad and long.

HINDQUARTERS Very powerful and well developed. Loin powerful, well let down in flank. Hocks low, stifles well bent and set straight.

FEET Large and round, well covered with hair.

TAIL Set low, well feathered, and carried about level with the back.

COAT Abundant, close, silky, and straight; legs well feathered.

COLOUR Plain white, with lemon markings, orange permissible; slight head markings and feckled muzzle, with white body preferred.

WEIGHT AND SIZE Dogs about 25–31·8kg (55–70lb); bitches about 20·4–27·2kg (45–60lb).

NOTE Male animals should have two apparently normal testicles fully descended into the scrotum.

SUSSEX SPANIEL

The Sussex spaniel is a rich golden liver colour and is the only spaniel to give tongue when hunting. The modern requirement that hunting shall be mute excludes the Sussex from competition, although his note is quite melodious and in heavily wooded Sussex country could be useful. The Sussex is shorter in the leg than the springers and a very slow hunter, and all these disabilities have led to his almost complete extinction. They were popular with shooting men in the late 1800s, but by the end of the Second World War there were only eight Sussex left in the world. That the breed still exists is due largely to the efforts of Mrs J. R. Freer who owned them.

Spaniel (Sussex)

GENERAL APPEARANCE Massive and strongly built. An active, energetic, strong dog, whose characteristic movement is a decided roll, and unlike that of any other spaniel.

HEAD AND SKULL The skull should be wide and show a moderate curve from ear to ear, neither flat nor apple headed, with a centre indentation and a pronounced stop. Brows frowning – occiput decided, but not pointed. Nostrils well developed and liver colour. A well balanced head.

EYES Hazel colour, fairly large, not too full, but soft expression and not showing the haw over much.

EARS Thick, fairly large and lobe shape, set moderately low but above eye level. Should lie closely, hair soft and wavy, but not too profuse.

MOUTH Strong and level, neither over- nor undershot, with a scissor bite.

NECK Long, strong and slightly arched, not carrying the head much above the level of the back. Not much throatiness, but well-marked frill.

FOREQUARTERS The shoulders should be sloping and free – arms well boned as well as muscular. Knees large and strong, pasterns short and well boned. Legs rather short and strong, moderately well feathered.

BODY Chest deep and well developed; not too round and wide. Back and loin well developed and muscular both in width and depth. The back ribs must be deep. Whole body should be strong and level with no sign of waistiness from aitches to hips.

HINDQUARTERS The thighs must be strongly boned as well as muscular; hocks large and strong, legs rather short and strong with good bone, moderately well feathered. The hind legs should not appear shorter than the fore legs, or be too much bent at the hocks so as to give a settery appearance, which is objectionable. The hind legs should be well feathered above the hocks, but not much hair below the hocks.

FEET Circular, well padded, well feathered between toes.

TAIL Set low and not carried above level of the back. Free actioned, thickly clothed with hair, but no feather. Docked from 5 to 7 in.

COAT Abundant and flat with no tendency to curl and ample undercoat for weather resistance.

COLOUR Rich golden liver and hair shading to gold at the tips; the gold predominating. Dark liver or puce is objectionable.

WEIGHT AND SIZE Ideal weight: dogs 20·4 kg (45 lb); bitches 18·2 kg (40 lb). Height 38–41 cm (15–16 in).

NOTE Male animals should have two apparently normal testicles fully descended into the scrotum.

FIELD SPANIEL

The field spaniel is a sad case of a dog for it was created by men to such an absurd specification that it practically died out. It is a product of crosses between Sussex spaniels and cockers, and the breeders' objective was to produce a long, low dog. So successful were they that dogs of enormous length and low enough to be referred to as 'drainpipes' emerged. The crossing with the golden coated Sussex produced colours which departed from the solid black and liver that had been their original colours. Now black and white, liver and white, and red or orange and white, while not disqualifying a dog, are considered faults.

It is interesting to see the breed emerging from the writings of 'Stonehenge'. In 1859 he said of field spaniels: 'Nowadays however only four distinct varieties are acknowledged in (a) the clumber (b) the Sussex (c) the Norfolk and (d) the modern cocker.' In 1867 he wrote that 'Among the Norfolk spaniels and mixed breeds are some black, black and tan and even liver coloured bred by a Mr Burdett.' In 1878 'Stonehenge' reported that 'much Sussex spaniel blood had been introduced by Mr Phineus Bullock.' Short legs and long bodies produced 'crooked legs and sagging backs,' to quote Roger Hall-Jones. The breed has hardly recovered from this early twentieth-century aberration. In 1949 one lonely dog was registered with the Kennel Club, but since then by inter-breeding with springers the numbers of field spaniels have increased considerably, and the quality has improved.

Spaniel (Field)

GENERAL APPEARANCE That of a well-balanced, noble, upstanding, sporting dog; built for activity and endurance; a combination of beauty and utility; of unusual docility.

HEAD AND SKULL The head should be characteristic as is that of the bulldog or the bloodhound; its very stamp and countenance should at once convey the impression of high breeding, character and nobility; skull well developed, with a distinct occiput protuberance, which gives the character alluded to; not too wide across the muzzle, long and lean, neither snipy nor squarely cut, and in profile curving gradually from nose to throat; lean beneath the eyes, a thickness here gives coarseness to the whole head. The great length of muzzle gives surface for the free development of the olfactory nerve, and thus secures the highest possible scenting powers. Nose, well developed, good with open nostrils.

EYES Not too full, but not small, receding or overhung. The colour in all cases to match the coat and markings, except in livers which

Irish water spaniel: Princhetts Astronut

Brittany spaniel: Narcisse Des Vivrays

may be a light hazel. Grave in expression suggesting docility and intelligence and showing no haw.

EARS Moderately long and wide, sufficiently clad with nice setter-like feather and set low. They should fall in graceful folds, the lower parts curling inwards and backwards.

MOUTH The jaws should be strong, with a perfect regular and complete scissor bite, i.e., the upper teeth closely overlapping the lower teeth and set square to the jaws.

NECK Long, strong and muscular, so as to enable the dog to retrieve his game without undue fatigue.

FOREQUARTERS The shoulders should be long and sloping and well set back, thus giving great activity and speed. The foreleg should be of fairly good length, with straight, clean, flat bone and nicely feathered. Immense bone is not desirable.

BODY Should be of moderate length, well ribbed up to a good strong loin, straight or slightly arched, never slack. The chest, deep and well developed, but not too round and wide. Back and loins very strong and muscular.

HINDQUARTERS Strong and muscular. The stifles should be moderately bent and not twisted either in or out.

FEET Not too small, round with short, soft hair between the toes; good strong pads.

TAIL Well set on and carried low, if possible below the level of the back, in a straight line or with a slight downward inclination, never elevated above the back, and in action always kept low, nicely fringed with wavy feather of silky texture.

COAT Flat or slightly waved, and never curly. Sufficiently dense to resist the weather and not too short. Silky in texture, glossy and refined without duffelness, curliness or wiriness. On the chest, under the belly and behind the legs, there should be abundant feather, but never too much, especially below the hocks, and that of the right sort – viz., setter-like.

COLOUR The field spaniel should be a self-coloured dog, viz. black, liver, golden liver, mahogany red, roan; or any of these colours with tan over the eyes, on the cheeks, feet and pasterns. Other colours, such as black and white, liver and white, red or orange and white, etc., while not debarring a dog, are faults.

WEIGHT AND SIZE About 16–23 kg (35–50½ lb). Height about 46 cm (18 in) at shoulder.

FAULTS Any departure from the foregoing points should be considered a fault, and the seriousness with which the fault is regarded should be in exact proportion to its degree.

NOTE Male animals should have two apparently normal testicles fully descended into the scrotum.

IRISH WATER SPANIEL

The Irish water spaniel is quite unlike any other spaniel. To start with, it walks in a manner 'peculiar to the breed', as the Kennel Club Standard says; then it is covered with 'dense, tight, crisp ringlets', and these curls 'have a natural oiliness', to quote the Standard again. It looks more like a retriever than a spaniel, and more like a poodle than either of them. It is possible to image it to be descended from Dr Johannes Caius's water spaniel of his book of 1550, which he described as being 'somewhat bigge and of a unensurable greatnesse, having long, rough and curled heare . . . notted from the shoulders to the hinder-most legges'. Or perhaps it comes down from the European water dog which is the ancestor of the poodle.

Early in the nineteenth century a Mr Justin McCarthy claimed to have invented the breed, but it seems most likely that he interbred from existing similar dogs and fixed the type. What is true is that his dog Boatswain, born in 1834, who lived for 18 years, sired an immense number of archetypal Irish water spaniels which were exported worldwide. The breed does very little field trialling but is a fine water dog, revelling in putting up and retrieving snipe and woodcock on boggy ground or dragging a greylag goose from fast-running water. It is powerful and has great powers of endurance. These dogs are not much seen but keep going with the discerning lone shooter and, despite their somewhat intractable coat, on the show bench.

Spaniel (Irish Water)

CHARACTERISTICS The gait, peculiar to the breed, differs from that of any other variety of spaniel.

GENERAL APPEARANCE The Irish water spaniel is a gundog bred for work in all types of shooting, and particularly suited for wild-fowling. His fitness for this purpose should be evident in his appearance; he is a strongly built, compact dog, intelligent, enduring and eager.

HEAD AND SKULL The head should be of good size. The skull high in dome, of good length and width sufficient to allow adequate brain capacity. The muzzle long, strong and somewhat square with a gradual stop. The face should be smooth and the skull covered with long curls in the form of a pronounced topknot growing in a well-defined peak to a point between the eyes. Nose large and well developed, dark liver colour. Withal there should be an impression of fineness.

EYES Comparatively small, medium to dark-brown colour, bright and alert.

EARS Very long and lobe-shaped in the leather, low set, hanging close to the cheeks and covered with long twisted curls of live hair.

MOUTH The jaws should be strong, with a perfect regular and complete scissor bite, i.e., the upper teeth closely overlapping the lower teeth and set square to the jaws.

NECK Strongly set into the shoulders, powerful, arching and long enough to carry the head well above the level of the back. The back and sides of the neck should be covered with curls similar to those on the body. The throat should be smooth, the smooth hair forming a V-shaped patch from the back of the lower jaw to the breast bone.

FOREQUARTERS The shoulders should be powerful and sloping. The chest deep and of large girth with ribs so well sprung behind the shoulders as to give a barrel-shaped appearance to the body but with normal width and curvature between the forelegs. The forelegs should be well boned and straight, with arms well let down and carrying the forearm at elbow and knee in a straight line with the point of the shoulder.

BODY Should be of good size. The back short, broad and level, strongly coupled to the hindquarters. The ribs carried well back. The loins deep and wide. The body as a whole being so proportioned as to give a barrel-shaped appearance accentuated by the springing of the ribs.

HINDQUARTERS Powerful with long well-bent stifles and hocks set low.

FEET Should be large and somewhat round and spreading; well covered with hair over and between the toes.

TAIL Peculiar to the breed, should be short and straight, thick at the root and tapering to a fine point. It should be low set, carried straight and below the level of the back; and in length should not reach the hock joint. Three to four inches of the tail at the root should be covered by close curls which stop abruptly; the remainder should be bare or covered by straight fine hairs.

COAT Should be composed of dense, tight, crisp ringlets free from woolliness. The hair should have a natural oiliness. The forelegs covered with feather in curls or ringlets down to the feet. The feather should be abundant all round, though shorter in front so as only to give a rough appearance. Below the hocks the hindlegs should be smooth in front, but feathered behind down to the feet.

COLOUR A rich dark liver having the purplish tint or bloom peculiar to the breed and sometimes referred to as puce-liver.

WEIGHT AND SIZE Height to the shoulders: dogs about 53–59 cm (21–23 in); bitches about 51–56 cm (20–22 in).

NOTE Male animals should have two apparently normal testicles fully descended into the scrotum.

THE BRITTANY SPANIEL

This dog, popular in France, other parts of Europe and America, is unknown in the U.K. but it is a splendid little gundog well described in the motto of the French Club de l'Epagneul Breton which is 'A maximum of quality for a minimum of size'. It has the spaniel characteristic of unflagging effort over long periods of hunting, but it differs from all other spaniels in a profound way, for it does not flush game – it points and it retrieves. It might therefore be regarded as a pointer/retriever in spite of its nomenclature.

In conformation the breed is longer in the leg than the English or Welsh springer and that, allied to the pointing instinct and predominantly red and white colouring, indicates a descent from the early setting spaniels with perhaps an infusion of setter. The Brittany Spaniel may be a very old breed going back to the Agassian dog of Britain which, we know from the Roman poet Oppian, was hunting hares in AD 150. The Welsh springer probably comes from the Agassian and always breeds true to that old dog's red and white colouring; and, such were the close historic trade links between Brittany and Wales, we can imagine the Brittany sharing common ancestry with the Welsh. The French assert that the Brittany comes from the Agassian and that the breed remained practically unknown doing their job in the middle of Brittany, whilst elsewhere French shooting men favoured English setters and pointers. They say that the dog was shaped in the Mountains of Arrée and that, like the terrain and the men from that hard region, they grow to be tough, rusticated and enduring.

The American Standard says that the colour should be 'Dark orange and white or liver and white. Any black in the coat, or a nose too dark in colour as to appear black, shall disqualify.' But the standard of the Club de l'Epagneul Breton, which succours the breed in its home country, includes (with orange and white, and liver and white) white and black, and tricolour. The tricolour of white, black and red is very popular in France in spite of the American objection. The existence of this black and white colouration (in contra-distinction to the invariable red and white Welsh) might indicate an infusion of English setter blood to produce both the black and the long legs.

It was a M. Arthur Enaud, a lawyer from Loudéac, who in 1907 founded the Club de l'Epagneul Breton and subsequently helped draw up the standard. Not until then did the little Brittany emerge from the shadows. The Club is very meticulous in protecting the breed's standard and, says M. Pouchain, its President, 'the breed must from time to time go back to the Mountains of Arrée to recover and conserve its type from an infusion of its original blood.'

This little bundle of compact energy is rightly growing very fast in popularity with gundog people in France and America.

American Kennel Club Standard
Brittany Spaniel

GENERAL APPEARANCE A compact, closely knit dog of medium size, a leggy spaniel having the appearance, as well as the agility, of a great ground coverer. Strong, vigorous, energetic and quick of movement. Not too light in bone, yet never heavy-boned and cumbersome. Ruggedness, without clumsiness, is a characteristic of the breed. So leggy is he that his height at the withers is the same as the length of his body. He has no tail, or at most not more than 4 in.

WEIGHT Should weigh between 30 and 40 lb.

HEIGHT $17\frac{1}{2}$–$20\frac{1}{2}$ in measured from the ground at the highest point of the shoulders. Any Brittany spaniel measuring under $17\frac{1}{2}$ in or over $20\frac{1}{2}$ in shall be disqualified from bench-show competition.

COAT Hair dense, flat or wavy, never curly. Not as fine as in other spaniel breeds, and never silky. Furnishings not profuse. The ears should carry a little fringe. Neither the front nor hind legs should carry heavy featherings. Note: long, curly, or silky hair is a fault. Any tendency toward excessive feathering should be severely penalised, as undesirable in a sporting dog which must face burrs and heavy cover.

SKIN Fine and fairly loose. (A loose skin rolls with briars and sticks, thus diminishing punctures or tearing. But a skin so loose as to form pouches is undesirable.)

COLOUR Dark orange and white, or liver and white. Some ticking is desirable, but not so much as to produce belton patterns. Roan patterns or factors of orange or liver shade are permissible. The orange or liver are found in standard parti-colour, or piebald patterns. Washed out or faded colours are desirable. Tri-colours (liver and white with some orange markings) are to be severely faulted. Any black in the coat, or a nose so dark in colour as to appear black, shall disqualify.

SKULL Medium length (approximately 4¾ in). Rounded, very slightly wedge-shaped, but evenly made. Width, not quite as wide as the length (about 4¾ in) and never so broad as to appear coarse, or so narrow as to appear racy. Well-defined, but gently sloping stop effect. Median line rather distinct. The occipital crest only apparent to the touch. Lateral walls well rounded. The Brittany should never be 'apple-headed' and he should never have an indented stop. (All measurements of skull are for a 19½ in dog.)

MUZZLE Medium length, about two thirds the length of the skull, measuring the muzzle from the tip to the stop, and the skull from the occipital crest to the stop between the eyes. Muzzle should taper gradually in both horizontal and vertical dimensions as it approaches the nostrils. Neither a Roman nose nor a concave curve (dish-face) is desirable. Never broad, heavy, or snipy.

NOSE Nostrils well open to permit deep breathing of air and adequate scenting while at top speed. Tight nostrils should be penalised. Never shiny. Colour fawn, tan, light shades of brown or deep pink. A black nose is a disqualification. A two-tone or butterfly nose should be severely penalised.

EYES Well set in head. Well protected from briars by a heavy, expressive eyebrow. A prominent, full or pop eye should be heavily penalised. It is a serious fault in a hunting dog that must face briars. Skull well chiselled under the eyes, so that the lower lid is not pulled back to form a pocket or haw for catching seeds, dirt and weed dust. Judges should check by forcing head down to see if lid falls away from the eye. Preference should be for darker-coloured eyes, though lighter shades of amber should not be penalised. Light and mean-looking eyes to be heavily penalised.

EARS Set high, above the level of the eyes. Short and leafy, rather than pendulous, reaching about half the length of the muzzle. Should lie flat and close to the head, with the tip rounded very slightly. Ears well covered with dense, but relatively short hair, and with little fringe.

LIPS Tight to the muzzle, with the upper lip overlapping the lower jaw only sufficient to cover under lip. Lips dry so that feathers do not stick. Drooling to receive a heavy penalty. Flews to be penalised.

TEETH Well-joined incisors. Posterior edge of upper incisors in contact with anterior edge of lower incisors, thus giving a true scissors bite. Overshot or undershot jaw to be penalised heavily.

NECK Medium length. Not quite permitting the dog to place his nose on the ground, without bending his legs. Free from throatiness, though not a serious fault unless accompanied by dewlaps. Strong, without giving the impression of being over-muscled. Well set into sloping shoulders. Never concave or ewe-necked.

BODY LENGTH Approximately the same as the height when measured at the withers. Body length is measured from the point of the forechest to the rear of the haunches. A long body should be heavily penalised.

WITHERS Shoulder blades should not protrude much. Not too widely set apart with perhaps two thumbs' width or less between the blades. At the withers, the Brittany is slightly higher than at the rump.

SHOULDERS Sloping and muscular. Blade and upper arm should form nearly a 90-degree angle when measured from the posterior point of the blade at the withers to the junction of the blade and upper arm, and thence to the point of the elbow nearest the ribs. Straight shoulders do not permit sufficient reach.

BACK Short and straight. Slight slope from highest point of withers to the root of the tail. Never hollow, saddle, sway, or roached-backed. Slight drop from hips to root of tail. Distance from last rib to upper thigh short, about three to four finger widths.

CHEST Deep, reaching the level of the elbow. Neither so wide nor so rounded as to disturb the placement of the shoulder bones and elbows, which causes a paddling movement, and often causes soreness from elbow striking ribs. Ribs well sprung, but adequate heart room provided by depth as well as width. Narrow or slab-sided chests are a fault.

FLANKS Rounded. Fairy full. Not extremely tucked up, nor yet flabby and falling. Loins short and strong. Narrow and weak loins are a fault. In motion the loin should not sway sideways, giving a zigzag motion to the back, wasting energy.

HINDQUARTERS Broad, strong and muscular, with powerful thighs and well-bent stifles, giving a hip set well into the loin and the marked angulation necessary for a powerful drive when in motion. Fat and falling hindquarters are a fault.

TAIL Naturally tailless, or not over 4 in long. (A tail substantially more than 4 in in length shall disqualify.) Natural or docked. Set on high, actually an extention of the spine at about the same level.

FRONT LEGS Viewed from the front, perpendicular, but not set too wide as in the case of a dog loaded in shoulder. Elbows and feet turning neither in or out. Viewed from the side, practically perpendicular to the pastern. Pastern slightly bent to give cushion to stride. Not so straight as in terriers. Falling pasterns, however, are a serious fault. Leg bones clean, graceful, but not too fine. An extremely heavy bone is as much a fault as spindly legs. One must look for substance and suppleness. Height to the elbows should approximately equal distance from elbow to withers.

HIND LEGS Stifles well bent. The stifle generally is the term used for knee joint. If the angle made by the upper and lower leg bones is too straight, the dog quite generally lacks drive, since his hind legs cannot drive as far forward at each stride as is desirable. However, the stifle should not be bent as to throw the hock joint far out behind the dog. Since factors not easily seen by the eye may give the dog his proper drive, a Brittany should not be condemned for straight stifle until the judge has checked the dog in motion from the side. When at a trot, the Brittany's hind foot should step into or beyond the print left by the front foot. The stifle joint should not turn out making a cow-hock. The cow-hock moves the foot out to the side, thus driving out of line, and losing reach at each stride. Thighs well feathers, but not profusely, halfway to the hock. Hocks, that is, the back pasterns, should be moderately short, pointing neither in nor out; perpendicular when viewed from the side. They should be firm when shaken by the Judge.

FEET Should be strong, proportionally smaller than other spaniels, with close-fitting, well-arched toes and thick pads. The Brittany is not 'up on his toes'. Toes not heavily feathered. Flat feet, splayed feet, paper feet, etc., are to be heavily penalised. An ideal foot is halfway between the hare- and cat-foot.

A guide to the Judge: the points below indicate only relative values. To be also taken into consideration are type, gait, soundness, spirit, optimum height, body length and general proportions.

SCALE OF POINTS Head (25). Body (35). Running gear (40). Total (100).

DISQUALIFICATIONS Any Brittany spaniel measuring under 17½ in or over 20½ in. Any black in the coat or a nose so dark in colour as to appear black. A tail substantially more than 4 inches in length.

N.B. The French Standard includes black and white and tricolour among the accepted colours.

CHAPTER THREE

Retrievers

The retriever as a specialised gundog did not exist until the late eighteenth century. Until then there were no shotguns, and game had mostly to be trapped or netted after hunting-up by setters or spaniels. The advent of the shotgun (and especially when the breach-loader superseded the slow muzzle-loader) quickened the art of 'shooting-flying', so that a great deal of game was shot and needed bringing to hand.

Setters had already been evolved from spaniels, and also in England were Newfoundland or St John's dogs imported through the port of Poole from vessels trading with Newfoundland. The smaller of these dogs with hard short coat, broad head and straight otter tail became known as the Labrador, and it is surprising that although these dogs were to hand in fair numbers and their qualities well known they were not immediately developed as retrievers to meet the new need. Thinking these dogs to be good water dogs (which they were) but not archetypal gundogs, sportsmen of the day crossed them with proven working dogs known to have good noses, such as setters, collies and water spaniels. From these matings emerged the wavy coated retriever. As breeding produced a less broken, less wavy coat the breed settled down to be known as flatcoats, and so they remain today. From around 1840 flatcoats were the ideal retrievers, but stalking up behind them came the Labrador whose ancestors had been much used to manufacture the flatcoat. Now as a pure breed in the hands of a few aristocrats they mounted an attack which, starting with the winning, in the first field trial entered by a Labrador, of a lowly Certificate of Merit by Mr Holland-Hibbert's Munden Single, quite overwhelmed the flatcoat opposition, so that practically every retriever championship since 1907 has been won by a Labrador, and the flatcoat has become a minority, though vigorous, breed.

When the championship has not been won by Labradors the winners have been golden retrievers which have won three times since 1907. They are another late nineteenth-century breed manufactured in 1868 (by the late Lord Tweedmouth) from a yellow flatcoat and a Tweed water spaniel whose mating produced four yellow puppies. In 1908 after the admixture of Labrador and Irish setter blood they first appeared in shows under the designation flatcoats (goldens) and they have been constantly used as retrievers ever since.

Two other retrievers manufactured from Labrador stock in the late nineteenth century which remain as minority breeds today are the curly coated retriever and the Chesapeake Bay retriever. The curly coated comes from a Labrador–water spaniel cross, and the Chesapeake Bay from Newfoundland via a shipwreck off Maryland. The curly coated is rare in England now, whilst the Chesapeake Bay is vigorous in America.

FLATCOAT RETRIEVER

The flatcoat was the first successful non-slip retriever manufactured to meet the new demand for a dog to collect game shot, and maybe wounded but not killed, following the introduction in 1830 of the shotgun with the percussion cap instead of the flintlock. This allowed shooting to become faster and therefore suited for use against driven birds and led to the growth of the *battue*. Victorian and Edwardian affluence especially amongst the aristocracy produced great shoots of almost unbelievable splendour and the need for retrievers to do much work on the thousands of birds slain. The first dog to come into popular prominence was the wavy coat. I think the basis of this dog, which in due course was to be known as the flatcoat, was the cross between the small dog imported from Newfoundland and known as the St John's dog or Labrador, and setters which were the pride of dogdom in the walking up of game which preceded the *battue*.

It must be admitted that the genesis of the flatcoat's bloodlines is obscure, for many crosses were tried, and Mr Shirley, one of the very important men in the history of the breed (he founded the Kennel Club at the age of 29), set out their genealogy thus in 1880: 'The various strains of wavy coated retrievers may be summarised as the Labrador type, the setter type, the collie type and the Russian type. To these must be, of course, added the various combinations of the above strains.' The flatcoat's reign came to an end from 1906 when the Labrador started its irresistible march, but both the black and liver colours still persist in the hands of enthusiasts. The flatcoat is an amusing dog. Its gait is rolling which is thought to come from the Newfoundland which worked off fishing boats. It takes a long

A flat-coat wet from the marsh

time to grow up and needs patience to train. He has been described thus in Dr Nancy Laughton's authoritative book: 'An Edwardian whose grace and distinction matched that of the epoch in which he had his heyday. His decline in favour was due partly to a gayness in youth that is combined with a slowness to mature and to take his responsibilities seriously.'

Retriever (Flatcoated)

GENERAL APPEARANCE A bright, active dog of medium size with an intelligent expression, showing power without lumber, and raciness without weediness.

HEAD AND SKULL The head should be long and nicely moulded. The skull flat and moderately broad. There should be a depression or stop between the eyes, slight and in no way accentuated, so as to avoid giving either a down or a dish-faced appearance. The nose of a good size, with open nostrils. The jaws should be long and strong, with a capacity of carrying a hare or pheasant.

EYES Should be of medium size, dark-brown or hazel, with a very intelligent expression (a round, prominent eye is a disfigurement) and they should not be obliquely placed.

EARS Should be small and well set-on, close to the side of the head.

NECK The head should be well set in the neck, which latter should be long and free from throatiness, symmetrically set and obliquely placed in shoulders running well into the back to allow of easily seeking for the trail.

FOREQUARTERS The chest should be deep and fairly broad, with a well-defined brisket, on which the elbows should work cleanly and evenly. The legs are of the greatest importance, the forelegs should be perfectly straight, with bone of good quality carried right down to the feet, and when the dog is in full coat the legs should be well feathered.

BODY The fore-ribs should be fairly flat, showing a gradual spring and well arched in the centre of the body, but rather lighter towards the quarters. Open couplings are to be ruthlessly condemned. The back should be short, square and well ribbed up.

HINDQUARTERS Should be muscular. The stifle should not be too straight or too bent, and the dog must neither be cow-hocked nor move too widely behind; in fact he must stand and move true on legs and feet all round. The legs should be well feathered.

FEET Should be round and strong with toes close and well arched, the soles being thick and strong.

TAIL Short, straight and well set on, carried gaily, but never much above the level of the back.

COAT Should be dense, of fine quality and texture, flat as possible.

COLOUR Black or liver.

WEIGHT AND SIZE Should be between 27·2 and 31·8 kg (60–70 lb).

NOTE Male animals should have two apparently normal testicles fully descended into the scrotum.

LABRADOR RETRIEVER

The Labrador came to England from Newfoundland at the beginning of the nineteenth century. By 1814 Col. Peter Hawker wrote *Instructions to a Young Sportsman*, in which he called the smaller of the two dogs that had arrived from Newfoundland 'the Labrador or St John's dog', saying it was 'by far the best for every kind of shooting'; so it had by then apparently started its gundog career. The dogs were brought by fishermen coming into Poole harbour, and an early purchaser was Lord Malmesbury who lived nearby. A handful of titled owners nurtured the breed along the English–Scottish borders, but their fame was unheralded when the advent of big *battues* of driven game called for the first non-slip retrievers. Eighteenth-century travellers to Newfoundland found no native dogs, so the breed must have been introduced from Europe where it had descended from the mastiff. Strangely, before it came to the fore as a retriever it had been used in the manufacture of the wavy coat, soon to be known as the flatcoat, which was regarded as the top retriever. When the Labrador, which had been kept pure and busily

Her master's bird – a fine cock pheasant retrieved by a yellow Labrador

A good delivery by a black Labrador

working by its influential patrons, entered the field trial scene from 1906 onwards it swept the flatcoat into oblivion and remains the top retriever today. It is good in water and thick cover, biddable, tender, sagacious, untiring and loyal and has a mouth of velvet and a superb nose. These characteristics keep it on top. Whether black is preferred to yellow is a matter of taste, for they can both win the championship.

Retriever (Labrador)

GENERAL APPEARANCE The general appearance of the Labrador should be that of a strongly built, short-coupled, very active dog, broad in the skull, broad and deep through the chest and ribs, broad and strong over the loins and hindquarters. The coat close, short with dense undercoat and free from feather. The dog must move neither too wide nor too close in front or behind; he must stand and move true all round on legs and feet.

HEAD AND SKULL The skull should be broad with a pronounced stop so that the skull is not in a straight line with the nose. The head should be clean cut without fleshy cheeks. The jaws should be medium length and powerful and free from snipiness. The nose wide and the nostrils well developed.

EYES The eyes, of medium size, expressing intelligence and good temper, should be brown or hazel.

EARS Should not be large and heavy and should hang close to the head, and set rather far back.

MOUTH Teeth should be sound and strong. The lower teeth just behind but touching the upper.

NECK Should be clean, strong and powerful and set into well placed shoulders.

FOREQUARTERS The shoulders should be long and sloping. The forelegs well boned and straight from the shoulder to the ground when viewed from either the front or side. The dog must move neither too wide nor too close in front.

BODY The chest must be of good width and depth with well-sprung ribs. The back should be short coupled.

HINDQUARTERS The loins must be wide and strong with well-turned stifles; hindquarters well developed and not sloping to the tail. The hocks should be slightly bent and the dog must neither be cow-hocked nor move too wide or too close behind.

FEET Should be round and compact with well-arched toes and well-developed pads.

TAIL The tail is a distinctive feature of the breed; it should be very thick towards the base, gradually tapering towards the tip, of medium length and practically free from any feathering, but clothed thickly all round with the Labrador's short thick dense coat, thus

A yellow Labrador brings back a rabbit from the salt marsh

giving that peculiar 'rounded' appearance which has been described as the 'otter' tail. The tail may be carried gaily, but should not curl over the back.

COAT The coat is another distinctive feature of the breed; it should be short and dense and without wave, with a weather-resisting undercoat, and should give a fairly hard feeling to the hand.

COLOUR The colour is generally black or yellow – but other whole colours are permitted. The coat should be free from any white markings, but a small white spot on the chest is allowable. The coat should be of a whole colour and not of a flecked appearance.

WEIGHT AND SIZE Desired height for dogs, 56–57 cm (22–22½ in); bitches 54–56 cm (21–22 in).

FAULTS Under- or overshot mouth; no undercoat; bad action; feathering; snipiness on the head; large or heavy ears; cow-hocked; tail curled over back.

NOTE Male animals should have two apparently normal testicles fully descended into the scrotum.

GOLDEN RETRIEVER

The beginnings of most gundogs are clouded in obscurity, but not that of the golden retriever, which is clearly set out by Edna Stone, who had access to the Tweedsmouth archives. It was created by Lord Tweedsmouth who brought his first yellow retriever in Brighton in 1865. It was called Nous. It was a yellow 'sport' from a litter of black wavy coats. Two years later his lordship got a Tweed water spaniel called Belle. This was probably light or liver coloured, as Tweed spaniels tended to be and in 1868 the mating of Nous and Belle produced four yellow puppies, Crocus, Cowslip, Primrose and Ada. At his home, Gaisachan, Lord Tweedmouth linebred from Cowslip by mating her in 1873 with another Tweed water spaniel, from which litter he kept a bitch puppy called Topsy who was of course three-quarters Tweed water spaniel. Then in 1876 Cowslip was mated with a red setter to produce a dog named Jack. These yellow retrievers were bred at Gaisachan until it was sold in 1905. When they were first shown at Crystal Palace in 1908 they were designated flatcoats (golden), for they shared the attributes of the flatcoat, and they continued to be so described until 1913 when they were called golden or yellow retrievers. In 1920 they were officially called golden retrievers.

The modern golden varies much in size and, in colour, ranges

Flatcoat retriever: Exclyst Cracksman

Golden retriever: Leighcourt Zobeide

Labrador retriever: F.T. Ch. Lambdale Shaun

Curly-coated retriever: Ch. Darelyn Fraser of Weavervale

Chesapeake Bay retriever: Ryshot Yank's Seastar of Arac

A golden retriever handing over a grouse

from cream to rust. They are the only dogs to keep alongside the Labrador in field trial successes, for the I.G.L. Championship has since 1908 been won always by a Labrador except for three golden triumphs and one inter-bred success. They are gay dogs with a very liquid gait. Their long coats need attention after a day in the field, and they can be obstinate in training; but they remain a welcome and currently popular member of the working retriever community.

Retriever (Golden)

GENERAL APPEARANCE Should be of a symmetrical, active, powerful dog, a good level mover, sound and well put together, with a kindly expression, not clumsy nor long in the leg.

HEAD AND SKULL Broad skull, well set on a clean and muscular neck, muzzle powerful and wide, not eark-jawed, good stop.

EYES Dark, set well apart, very kindly in expression, with dark rims.

EARS Well proportioned, of moderate size, and well set on.

MOUTH Teeth should be sound and strong. Neither overshot nor undershot, the lower teeth just behind but touching the upper.

A golden retriever clearing barbed wire with a pheasant

NECK The neck should be clean and muscular.

FOREQUARTERS The forelegs should be straight with good bones. Shoulders should be well laid back and long in the blade.

BODY Well balanced, short coupled, and deep through the heart. Ribs deep and well sprung.

HINDQUARTERS The loins and legs should be strong and muscular, with good second thighs and well-bent stifles. Hocks well let down, not cow-hocked.

FEET Round and cat-like, not open nor splay.

TAIL Should not be carried too gay nor curled at the tip.

COAT Should be flat or wavy with good feathering, and dense water-resisting undercoat.

COLOUR Any shade of gold or cream, but neither red nor mahogany. The presence of a few white hairs on chest permissible. White collar, feet, toes or blaze should be penalised. Nose should be black.

WEIGHT AND SIZE The average weight in good hard conditions should be: dogs, 32–37 kg (70–80 lb); bitches, 27–32 kg (60–70 lb). Height at shoulder: dogs 56–61 cm (22–24 in); bitches 51–56 cm (20–22 in).

NOTE Male animals should have two apparently normal testicles fully descended into the scrotum.

CURLY-COATED RETRIEVER

This dog was made to meet the demand for retrievers which arose after the introduction of the percussion cap in 1830. Retrievers of the time were produced by crossing any two likely gundogs. In full flood were setters, spaniels and pointers, and Labradors. The curly-coated must come from some early poodle ancestor, for he is covered in a crisp Astrakhan coat of dense black or liver curls. A cross between the then unsung small Labrador or St John's dog and the Irish water spaniel may have produced him, but the poodle was used as an outcross well into the nineteenth century. This would not be to the breed's working disadvantage, for the old poodle was a gundog. The breed has been eliminated in field trials by the wavy coat in 1880 and by the Labrador early in the twentieth century but is recognised, by its few enthusiasts, as a strong retriever, superb in water as befits its standard height of 25–27 in compared with the labrador's 22 in. The breed matures slowly which leads inexperienced trainers to think it pig-headed as does its rather independent attitude of mind. Not until three years old is a curly-coated likely to be a mature gundog, and that is quite a wait for a man eager to be accompanied by a dog out shooting.

Retriever (Curly-Coated)

GENERAL APPEARANCE A strong smart upstanding dog showing activity, endurance and intelligence.

HEAD AND SKULL Long well-proportioned flat skull, jaws strong and long but not inclined to snipiness. Nose black in the black-coated variety with wide nostrils, coarseness of head to be deprecated.

EYES Black or brown but not 'gooseberry' coloured, rather large but not too prominent.

EARS Rather small, set on low, lying close to the head and covered with short curls.

MOUTH Teeth strong and level.

NECK Should be moderately long, free from throatiness.

FOREQUARTERS Shoulders should be very deep, muscular and well laid back.

HINDQUARTERS Strong and muscular, hock low to the ground with good bend to stifle and hock.

BODY Well-sprung ribs, good depth of brisket, not too long in the loins, as little tucked-up in flank as possible.

FEET Round and compact with well-arched toes.

TAIL Moderately short, carried fairly straight and covered with curls, tapering towards the point, gay tail not desirable.

COAT Should be one mass of crisp small curls all over. This being the main characteristic of the breed should be given great consideration when making judging awards.

COLOUR Black or liver.

WEIGHT AND SIZE 31·8–36·3 kg (70–80 lb). Approximately 63–69 cm (25–27 in).

FAULTS Wide skull, light eyes, curled tail and bad movement.

NOTE Male animals should have two apparently normal testicles fully descended into the scrotum.

THE CHESAPEAKE BAY RETRIEVER

This dog was bred from two Newfoundland puppies, a red dog and a black bitch, shipwrecked off Maryland in 1807 and rescued by the American ship *Canton*. After being presented to the man who looked after the shipwrecked mariners they were crossed with other gundogs. The resulting progeny after 75 years of experiment became a fixed breed which was named after Chesapeake Bay, in whose icy Atlantic waters they were famous for retrieving duck. They developed a coat to withstand these icy conditions and became a duck hunter's favourite, prepared to be, for long periods, in the water fetching hundreds of duck in a day. The yellow coat varies from gingery brown to faded straw, and its texture is a great feature being a mixture of Labrador straightness and flatcoat waviness. It is a rough coat with a dense woolly protective undercoat and is wavy over shoulders, neck, back and loins, whilst the stern and tail are feathered. That is what the American Standard says of its 'dead grass'-coloured coat which is so important in allowing the dog to shake off water with one shrug after a long immersion, resisting the water, says the Standard, 'in the same way that a duck's feathers do'. For its specialised purpose this big, strong dog takes some beating but it is not much favoured by modern shooting men.

American Kennel Club Standard
Chesapeake Bay Retriever

HEAD Skull broad and round with medium stop, nose medium, short muzzle, pointed but not sharp. Lips thin, not pendulous. Ears small, set well up on head, hanging loosely and of medium leather. Eyes medium large, very clear, of yellowish colour and wide apart.

NECK Of medium length with a strong muscular appearance, tapering to shoulders.

SHOULDER, CHEST AND BODY Shoulders, sloping and should have full liberty of action with plenty of power without any restrictions of movement. Chest strong, deep and wide. Barrel round and deep. Body of medium length, neither cobby nor roached, but rather approaching hollowness, flanks well tucked up.

BACK QUARTERS AND STIFLES Back quarters should be as high as or a trifle higher than the shoulders. They should show fully as much power as the forequarters. There should be no tendency to weakness in either fore or hindquarters. Hindquarters should be especially powerful to supply the driving power for swimming. Back should be short, well-coupled and powerful. Good hindquarters are essential.

LEGS, ELBOWS, HOCKS AND FEET Legs should be medium length and straight, showing good bone and muscle, with well-webbed hare-feet of good size. The toes well rounded and close, pasterns slightly bent and both pasterns and hocks medium length – the straighter the legs the better. Dewclaws, if any, must be removed from the hind legs. Dewclaws on the forelegs may be removed. A dog with dewclaws on the hind legs must be disqualified.

STERN Tail should be medium length – varying from: dogs, 12–15 in, and bitches 11–14 in; medium heavy at base, moderate feathering on stern and tail permissible.

COAT AND TEXTURE Coat should be thick and short, nowhere over $1\frac{1}{2}$ in long, with a dense fine woolly undercoat. Hair on face and legs should be very short and straight with tendency to wave on the shoulders, neck, back and loins only. The curly coat or coat with a tendency to curl not permissible.

WEIGHT Dogs 65–75 lb; bitches 55–65 lb. Height: Dogs 23–26 in; bitches 21–24 in.

SYMMETRY AND QUALITY The Chesapeake dog should show a

bright and happy disposition and an intelligent expression, with general outlines impressive and denoting a good worker. The dog should be well proportioned, a dog with a good coat and well balanced in other points being preferable to the dog excelling in some but weak in others. The texture of the dog's coat is very important, as the dog is used for hunting under all sorts of adverse weather conditions, often working in ice and snow. The oil in the harsh outer coat and woolly undercoat is of extreme value in preventing the cold water from reaching the dog's skin and aids in quick drying. A Chesapeake's coat should resist the water in the same way that a duck's feathers do. When he leaves the water and shakes himself, his coat should not hold the water at all, being merely moist. Colour and coat are extremely important, as the dog is used for duck hunting. The colour must be as nearly that of his surroundings as possible and with the fact that dogs are exposed to all kinds of adverse weather conditions, often working in ice and snow, the colour of coat and its texture must be given every consideration when judging on the bench or in the ring. Courage, willingness to work, alertness, nose intelligence, love of water, general quality, and, most of all, disposition, should be given primary consideration in the selection and breeding of the Chesapeake Bay dog.

APPROXIMATE MEASUREMENTS (in inches) Length head, nose to occiput (9½ to 10). Girth at ears (20 to 21). Muzzle below eyes (10 to 10½). Length of ears (4½ to 5). Width between eyes (2½ to 2¾). Girth neck close to shoulder (20 to 22). Girth of chest to elbows (35 to 36). Girth at flank (24 to 25). Length from occiput to tail base (34 to 35). Girth forearms at shoulders (10 to 11). Girth upper thigh (19 to 20). From root to root of ear, over skull (5 to 6). Occiput to top shoulder blades (9 to 9½). From elbow to elbow over the shoulders (25 to 26).

DISQUALIFICATIONS Black or liver coloured. Dewclaws on hind legs. White on any part of body, except breast, belly or spots on feet. Feathering on tail or legs over 1¾ in long. Undershot, overshot or any deformity. Coat curly or tendency to curl all over body. Specimens unworthy or lacking in breed characteristics.

POSITIVE SCALE OF POINTS Head, including lips, ears and eyes (16). Neck (4). Shoulders and body (12). Back quarters and stifles (12). Elbows, legs and feet (12). Colour (4). Stern and tail (10). Coat and texture (18). General conformation (12). Total (100). Note: the question of coat and general type of balance takes precedence over any scoring table which could be drawn up.

CHAPTER FOUR

Pointers and Setters

Pointers and setters go together as a group because their functions are similar. Their job is to hunt across a wide front on moor or stubbles covering big distances with their galloping stride and, with head and nostrils held high across the wind, to scent game and, standing rigid, to locate its scent by pointing or setting. These two functions are the same, but the pointer stands to the point whilst the setter may crouch; this is instinctive from the days when, before guns were invented, they 'sat' (and that is the derivation of the name 'setter') and lay down pointing the covey and waiting for the hunter to creep up and throw a net over both dog and birds. These dogs were once used to retrieve, but now their function ends when the bird is flushed and shot and the rest of the covey moved into the air from their seat. Some trainers still teach pointers and setters to retrieve; but it is not instinctive in them so to do, and harsh forced methods are frequently used. The fact is, though, that in America hunters wanting to use only one dog capable of wide ranging and pointing do teach pointers and setters to retrieve so that they can be out with only one dog both to locate and to retrieve game. I think they would do better to use a pointer-retriever for this purpose; but man has taught dogs many skills over the centuries, and I suppose that if enough setters are trained to retrieve we will finish up with setter-retrievers. The skeleton of a dog found at a Neolithic site at Windmill Hill near Avebury in Wiltshire appears to have all the characters of a pointer which means that the pointer has been in England since at least 2000 BC. But it would seem though that they were not adapted for sport and were unknown in the field until the eighteenth century.

Modern pointers came out of Spain to England, according to William Arkwright in *The Pointer and his Predecessors*, brought by returning officers from the war of the Spanish Succession after the Peace of Utrecht in 1713. In England, in the next 100 years, they were bred to a wonderfully high standard, becoming in the process lighter and faster. Such was the perfection of these dogs that they went back to their country of origin to envious hunters on the

Continent, a great compliment to English dog breeders of that era.

The original Spanish imports were slow heavy cumbersome dogs, and to get the lighter faster animals that British breeders wanted various crosses were tried with foxhounds, greyhounds and bull terriers. But too much outcrossing reduced the pointing instinct, and the old pointer blood had to be brought back into these cross-breeds to produce the wonderful dogs they became by the nineteenth century when their popularity and usefulness were at their height.

Setting dogs are of some antiquity and are known to have been used for sport in France in the twelfth century and are known, too, to have come to France from Spain. Because of the country of origin the French called them '*espaignolz*', and so when they came to England they were called 'spaniels'. All setters were bred from spaniels which were the first 'setting' dogs. Today setter and spaniel heads show clearly their common ancestry, and a big springer looks not unlike a setter, for setters were bred from long-legged spaniels until their type was fixed. Greyhounds, foxhounds and pointers were used to give setters speed and nose, but today the long-legged setter needs no outcross to improve either its appearance or its looks. Alas! opportunities for pointers and setters to work have reduced over the years with the advent of the sport of driving grouse and partridges over static guns, so that many breeds have been for long years in the hands of breeders for showing and for the pet market. There are pockets of field trial breeders and trainers, though, and as the cost of driving game mounts it may be that walking behind pointing and setting dogs will be found to be economically attractive as well as an enjoyable skill. This handful of dedicated field trial adherents may prove the saviour of the breeds and present to the walking guns strains of dogs ready to be expanded to meet their new-found old-fashioned needs. Perhaps shooters will experience again the thrill of watching these dogs criss-crossing their ground or, as Arkwright put it, 'The chief glory of the sport is to shoot over a brace of racing pointers, matched for speed and style, sweeping over the rough places like swallows and passing each other as if they were fine ladies not introduced.'

THE POINTER

The beginnings of the pointer were most fully researched by Arkwright in his book *The Pointer and his Predecessors.* He was looking for references to the pointer in old literature, and the earliest

Dr J. B. Maurice at a field trial with his English setter bitch Downsmans Tormentil

mention that he found came from Italy in the thirteenth century which referred to 'brachs with falling ears which know of beasts and birds by the scent, therefore they are useful for sporting'. Archaeological evidence, not available to Arkwright, places dogs of the pointer type alongside the peoples of the Neolithic migrations across Europe around 3000 BC, and the remains of the Windmill Hill dog dating from 2000 BC, found near Avebury in Wiltshire, have been identified as being of a pointer type. Arkwright found that pointers were used with the hawk and net in France, Spain and Italy in the seventeenth century but decided that they were first brought to England from Spain, their place of origin, by officers returning after the Peace of Utrecht in 1713. This Spanish pointer was a heavy slow dog, and over the next 100 years careful breeding in England produced a lighter faster animal ideal for hunting and pointing walked-up game. To achieve this transformation crossing with foxhound and greyhound was resorted to, and of the splendidly athletic result Arkwright wrote: 'I glory that his worth is today acclaimed by the whole sporting world; even Italy, France and Spain, the very countries that have contributed to his manufacture, vying with each other in the cult of the British pointer.'

A pointer on point

A pointer being cast off by its handler

With the advent of stubbles reaped short, root crops drilled in rows instead of broadcast, so that partridges could flee along the straight rows, and the increasing popularity of shooting driven birds, the pointer's use has much diminished over the last 75 years. There still are dogging grouse moors on which they may be set to range with their long stride and high-held nostrils, but though the pointer is still in good and keen hunting hands it is of minor importance in the field compared with its heyday early in the nineteenth century.

Pointer

CHARACTERISTICS The pointer should be symmetrical and well built all over. Alert, with the appearance of strength, endurance and speed.

HEAD AND SKULL The skull should be medium breadth and in

proportion to the length of foreface; the stop well defined, pronounced occipital bone. Nose and eye-rims dark, but may be lighter in the case of a lemon and white-coloured dog. The nostrils wide, soft and moist. The muzzle somewhat concave, and ending on a level with the nostrils, giving a slightly dish-faced appearance. The cheek-bones should not be prominent. Well-developed soft lip.

EYES The same distance from the occiput as from the nostrils. A slight depression under the eyes, which should be bright and kindly in expression, not bold or staring, and not looking down the nose. The colour of the eyes either hazel or brown according to the colour of the coat.

MOUTH Scissors bite, neither under- nor overshot.

NECK Long, muscular, slightly arched, springing cleanly from the shoulders and free from throatiness.

EARS The ears should be set on fairly high, and lie close to the head; they should be of medium length, and inclined to be pointed at the tips.

FOREQUARTERS The shoulders long, sloping and well laid back. The chest just wide enough for plenty of heart room. The brisket well let down, to a level with the elbows. The forelegs straight and firm, of good oval bone, with the back sinews strong and visible. The knee joint should be flat with the front of the leg, and protrude very little on the inside. Pasterns lengthy, strong and resilient.

BODY Well-sprung ribs, gradually falling away at the loin, which should be strong, muscular and slightly arched. The couplings short. The haunch bones well spaced and prominent, but not above the level of the back. The general outline from head to tail being a series of graceful curves, giving a strong but lissom appearance.

HINDQUARTERS Well-turned stifles. The hock should be well let down, and close to the ground. A good expanse of thigh, which should be very muscular, as should also the second thighs.

FEET The feet oval, with well-knit arched toes, well cushioned underneath.

GAIT Smooth, covering plenty of ground with each stride. Driving hind action, elbows turning neither in nor out. Definitely not a hackney action.

TAIL The tail of medium length, thick at the root, growing gradually thinner to the point. It should be well covered with close hair, and carried on a level with the back, with no upward curl. With the dog in movement the tail should lash from side to side.

COAT The coat should be fine, short, hard and evenly distributed, perfectly smooth and straight, with a decided sheen.

COLOUR The usual colours are lemon and white, orange and white, liver and white, and black and white. Self colours and tri-colours are also correct.

SIZE Desirable heights: dogs 63–69 cm (25–27 in); bitches 61–66 cm (24–26 in).

NOTE Male animals should have two apparently normal testicles fully descended into the scrotum.

THE ENGLISH SETTER

The English setter was without doubt bred from spaniel stock: spaniels were setting game and known as setters in 1576 when Johannes Caius wrote his treatise *Of Englishe Dogges*, for one of the breeds of which he wrote was 'the Dogge called the Setter', and he describes very fully its technique of setting partridges and quail to the net. When game had to be located in open spaces, like moors or stubbles, speed was required to range over a lot of country sparsely populated with game; so by selection from long-legged dogs a taller, thinner, faster dog was separated out from the heavy spaniel.

The most copiously recorded history of the English setter comes from Edward Laverack whose tombstone reads: 'To the memory of Edward Laverack; born Keswich 1800; died at Broughall Cottage, 1877. This monument is erected by admirers in England and America'. In 1825 he got Old Moll and Ponto, and on them he based his line. He was so successful with constant inbreeding that the English setter he described as 'coloured blue or red belton, that is dogs with a white background and densely ticked with black or lemon,' became known throughout the world as the Laverack setter. A French gundog man in 1978 told me that he had just lost the best gundog he had ever owned. '*C'était un Laverack*,' he said. Laverack asserted that Old Moll and Ponto came from the Rev. A. Harrison of Carlisle and said that in these hands they had been bred pure for 35 years, i.e. since 1790. What we would all like to know but has never been revealed is the Rev. Harrison's starting point 30 years earlier than Old Moll and Ponto. Starting with Laverack blood another famous kennel grew under Mr R. Ll. Purcell Llewellin. He is said to have rid the breed of the heaviness and feather brain that Laverack's inbreeding produced. Llewellin died in 1925, and all his dogs were bought for £1,600 by a Mr Humphreys who carried the Llewellin flag forward and imported 33 dogs of Llewellin strain back into Britain from America where the line had flourished and indeed where they had been registered as Llewellin setters.

Two promising English setter pups

The English setter is a lovely dog and now more in the hands of breeders for the show than for field sports; but it is still used on the moors and still competes in field trials. It could have a future.

English Setter

CHARACTERISTICS An intensely friendly and quiet-natured dog with a keen game sense.

GENERAL APPEARANCE Of medium height, clean in outline, elegant in appearance and movement.

HEAD AND SKULL Head should be long and reasonably lean, with a well-defined stop. The skull oval from ear to ear, showing plenty of brain room, and with a well-defined occipital protuberance. The muzzle moderately deep and fairly square; from the stop to the point of the nose should equal the length of skull from occiput to eyes; the nostrils wide and the jaws of nearly equal length; flews not to be too pendulous; the colour of the nose should be black or liver, according to the colour of the coat.

EYES The eyes should be bright, mild and intelligent, and of a dark hazel colour, the darker the better.

EARS The ears of moderate length, set on low, and hanging in neat folds close to the cheek; the tip should be velvety, the upper part clothed in fine silky hair.

MOUTH The jaws should be strong, with a perfect regular and complete scissor bite, i.e. the upper teeth closely overlapping the lower teeth and set square to the jaws.

NECK Neck should be rather long, muscular and lean, slightly arched at the crest, and clean cut where it joins the head; towards the shoulder it should be larger, and very muscular, not throaty or pendulous below the throat, but elegant in appearance.

FOREQUARTERS The shoulders should be well set back or oblique; the chest should be deep in the brisket, and of good depth and width between the shoulder blades. The forearm big and very muscular, with rounded bone, and elbow well let down, pasterns short, muscular, round and straight.

BODY The body should be of moderate length, the back short and level with good round widely sprung ribs and deep in the back ribs, i.e. well ribbed up.

HINDQUARTERS The loins should be wide, slightly arched, strong and muscular, with defined second thigh. Stifles well bent and rugged, thighs long from hip to hock.

FEET The feet should be very close and compact and well protected by hair between the toes.

TAIL The tail should be set on almost in line with the back; medium length, not curly or ropy, to be slightly curved or scimitar-shaped but with no tendency to turn upwards; the flat or feather hanging in long pendant flakes. The feather should not commence at the root, but slightly below, and increase in length to the middle, then gradually taper off towards the end; the hair long, bright, soft and silky, wavy, but not curly.

COAT The coat from the back of the head in a line with the ears ought to be slightly wavy, long and silky, which should be the case with the coat generally; the breeches and forelegs, nearly down to the feet, should be well feathered.

COLOUR The colour may be either black and white, lemon and white, liver and white or tricolour – that is black, white and tan; those without heavy patches of colour on the body, but flecked all over, preferred.

WEIGHT AND SIZE Height: dogs 65–68 cm (25½–27 in); bitches 61–65 cm (24–25½ in). Weight: dogs 27–30 kg (60–66 lb); bitches 25–28 kg (55–61½ lb).

FAULTS Any departure from the foregoing points should be considered a fault, and the seriousness with which the fault is regarded should be in exact proportion to its degree.

NOTE Male animals should have two apparently normal testicles fully descended into the scrotum.

THE IRISH SETTER

The Irish setter had, wrote 'Stonehenge' in the 1850s, 'a prejudice existing against them in England where they were supposed to be difficult to break, and always inclined to be unsteady'. But he thought that the dog had overcome this prejudice 'and now takes his share of the work on Scotch and Welsh moors as well as on his native mountains'.

The Irish setter has suffered over the years for being so beautiful. He has been bred for the pet market too widely for his well-being. It seems most likely that the breed came from the red and white spaniel, and a case can be made for tracing his ancestry back to the long-legged Brittany spaniel which is a pointer to this day. Selective breeding has got rid of the white except for a variety of small white patches allowed nowadays by the standards. It is the persistence of these white spots which indicates the type of its forebears and, in nineteenth-century shows, there were more classes for red and white setters than for pure reds. The most important influence on the breed came from Mrs I. Nagle who won the Championship first in 1927 and had won it 17 times by 1961 when she retired from trialling. Her kennel name was Fulhamstead, and all working Irish setters will almost certainly have that name in their pedigree.

Irish Setter

GENERAL APPEARANCE Must be racy, full of quality, and kindly in expression.

HEAD AND SKULL The head should be long and lean, not narrow or snipy, and not coarse at the ears. The skull oval (from ear to ear), having plenty of brain room, and with well-defined occipital protuberance. Brows raised, showing stop. The muzzle moderately deep, and fairly square at end. From the stop to the point of the nose should be long, the nostrils wide, and the jaws of nearly equal length, flews not to be pendulous. The colour of the nose dark mahogany, or dark walnut, or black.

EYES Should be dark hazel or dark brown and ought not to be too large.

Pointer: Ch. Toberdoney Prince Consort

English setter: F.T. Ch. Sharnberry Tern

Irish setter: F.T. Ch. Franko of Crowhill

EARS The ears should be of moderate size, fine in texture, set on low, well back; and hanging in a neat fold close to the head.

MOUTH Not over- or undershot.

NECK Should be moderately long, very muscular, but not too thick, slightly arched, free from all tendency to throatiness.

FOREQUARTERS The shoulders to be fine at the points, deep and sloping well back. The chest as deep as possible, rather narrow in front. The forelegs should be straight and sinewy, having plenty of bone, with elbows free, well let down, not inclined either in or out.

BODY Should be proportionate, the ribs well sprung, leaving plenty of lung room. Loins muscular, slightly arched.

HINDQUARTERS Should be wide and powerful. The hind legs from hip to hock should be long and muscular; from hock to heel short and strong. The stifle and hock joints well bent, and not inclined either in or out.

FEET Should be small, very firm, toes strong, close together and arched.

TAIL Should be of moderate length, proportionate to the size of the body, set on rather low, strong at root, and tapering to a fine point; to be carried as nearly as possible on a level with or below the back.

COAT AND FEATHERING On the head, front of the legs, and tips of the ears, should be short and fine, but on all other parts of the body and legs it ought to be of moderate length, flat, and as free as possible from curl or wave. The feather on the upper portion of the ears should be long and silky; on the back of fore and hind legs should be long and fine; a fair amount of hair on the belly, forming a nice fringe, which may extend on chest and throat. Feet to be well feathered between the toes. Tail to have a nice fringe of moderately long hair, decreasing in length as it approaches the point. All feathering to be as straight and as flat as possible.

COLOUR The colour should be rich chestnut, with no trace whatever of black; white on chest, throat, chin or toes, or a small star on the forehead, or a narrow streak or blaze on the nose or face not to disqualify.

NOTE Male animals should have two apparently normal testicles fully descended into the scrotum.

THE GORDON SETTER

There is no doubt where the Gordon setter got its name. It is named after Alexander, fourth Duke of Gordon (1743–1827).

Until its present name was adopted in 1924 it was known as the Black and Tan setter. In the first field trial ever held in 1865 Gordon setters took the first three places; but they fell into disfavour in Britain in spite of their considerable success in Norway, France and America to which country a pair, Rake and Rachel, went from Gordon Castle in 1842. By 1883 registrations at the Kennel Club showed that of 116 Gordons registered 76 came from France and five from other parts of the Continent. Isaac Sharpe, a man of great influence on gundogs from the late 1800s to his death in 1938, was the leading influence on Gordons of which his kennel contained up to 60 dogs.

Gordons have the reputation of being more easily trained than English or Irish setters and they have the most spectacular coat, shining coal-black with marks of a rich warm mahogany tan which comes from past outcrossing with the Irish setter.

Once upon a time they had a lot of white in their colouration; but that has been bred out, and now only a very small white spot on the chest is acceptable. The Gordon is the heaviest of the setters and has a reputation of being strong enough to go all day without flagging.

Gordon Setter

GENERAL APPEARANCE A stylish dog, built on galloping lines, having a thoroughbred appearance consistent with its build which can be compared to a weight-carrying hunter. Must have symmetrical conformation throughout, showing true balance. Strong, fairly short and level back. Shortish tail. Head fairly long, clearly lined and with intelligent expression, clear colours and long falt coat.

HEAD AND SKULL Head deep rather than broad, but definitely broader than the muzzle, showing brain room. Skull slightly rounded and broadest between the ears. The head should have a clearly indicated stop, and length from occiput to stop should be slightly longer than from stop to nose. Below and above the eyes should be lean and the cheeks as narrow as the leanness of the head allows. The muzzle should be fairly long with almost parallel lines and not pointed, as seen from above or from the side. The flews not pendulous but with clearly indicated lips. Nose big and broad, with open nostrils and black in colour. The muzzle should not be quite as deep as its length.

EYES Of fair size, not too deep nor too prominent but sufficiently under the brows to show keen and intelligent expression. Dark brown and bright.

EARS Set low on the head and lying close to it, of medium size and thin.

MOUTH Must be even and not under- nor overshot.

NECK Long, lean and arched to the head and without any throatiness.

FOREQUARTERS Shoulders should be long and slope well back; with wide flat bone and fairly close at withers; should not be loaded, i.e. too thick, which interferes with liberty of movement. Elbows well let down and showing well under the body, which gives freedom of action. Forelegs big, flat-boned and straight, with strong upright pasterns, well feathered.

BODY Of moderate length, deep in brisket, with ribs well sprung. Deep in back ribs, i.e. well ribbed up. Loins wide and slightly arched. Chest not too broad.

HINDQUARTERS Hind legs from hip to hock should be long, broad and muscular; hock to heel short and strong, stifles well bent; hocks straight, not inclined either in or out. Pelvis should tend to the horizontal, i.e. opposite of goose rump.

FEET Oval, with close-knit, well-arched toes, with plenty of hair between. Full toe pads and deep heel cushions.

TAIL Fairly short, straight or slightly scimitar-shaped and should not reach below the hocks. Carried horizontal or below line of back. Thick at the root tapering to a fine point. The feather or flat which starts near the root should be long and straight, and growing shorter uniformly to the point.

COAT On the head and front of legs and tips of ears should be short and fine, but on all other parts of the body and legs it ought to be of moderate length, fairly flat and as free as possible from curl or wave. The feather on the upper portion of the ears should be long and silky, on the back of the hind legs long and fine; a fair amount of hair on the belly forming a nice fringe which may extend on chest and throat. All feathering to be as flat and straight as possible.

COLOUR Deep shining coal-black, with no sign of rustiness, with tan markings of a rich chestnut red, i.e. colour of a ripe horse-chestnut as taken from shell. Tan should be lustrous. Black pencilling allowed on toes and also black streak under jaw. *Tan markings*: two clear spots over the eyes not over three-quarters of an inch in diameter. On the sides of the muzzle, the tan should not reach above the base of nose, resembling a stripe around the end of the muzzle from one side to the other. On the throat. Two large clear spots on the chest. On this inside of the hind legs and inside the thighs showing down the front of the stifle and broadening out to the outside of the hind legs from the hock to the toes. It must, however, not completely eliminate the black on the back of the hind legs. On the forelegs, up to the elbows behind, and to the knees or a little above, in front. Around the vent. A white spot on chest is allowed but the smaller the better.

WEIGHT AND SIZE As a guide to size, shoulder height for males 66 cm (26 in) and weight about 29·5 kg (65 lb); females, 62 cm (24 in) and weight about 25·4 kg (56 lb), in show condition.

FAULTS General impression: unintelligent appearance, the bloodhound type with heavy and big head and ears and clumsy body; the collie type with pointed muzzle and curved tail. The Head: pointed, snipy, down- or upturned muzzle, too small or large mouth. The Eyes: too light in colour, too deep set or too prominent. The Ears: set too high, or unusually broad or heavy. The Neck: thick and short. Shoulders and Back: irregularly formed. The Chest: too broad. The Legs and Feet: crooked legs, out-turned elbows. The toes scattered, flat footed. The Tail too long, badly carried or hooked at the end. The Coat: curly, like wool, not shining. The Colour: yellow, or straw-coloured tan, or without clearly defined lines between the different colours. White feet. Too much white on the chest. In the black there should be no tan hairs.

NOTE Male animals should have two apparently normal testicles fully descended into the scrotum.

CHAPTER FIVE

Pointer-Retrievers

This group of dogs all come from the continent of Europe and most of them from Germany. The exception is the Vizsla, which comes from Hungary, but hunting conditions in Hungary were similar to those in Germany which dictated the necessity of breeding these all-round dogs to perform a range of tasks encompassed by no other gundog. They are bred to be capable of hunting and pointing like pointers and setters, hunting and flushing like spaniels and retrieving like spaniels and retrievers. It was the great variety of game and country which called for the creation of these dogs capable of accompanying a single hunter to seek out and indicate game and retrieve it from very diverse country and from water. These dogs are a mixture of local pointer, foxhound, English pointer and braque blood, and they are bred for wide ranging and stamina. They have proved a great success all over the world especially when rapid movement from duck to pheasant, hare to duck and goose to snipe is the order of the day.

THE GERMAN SHORT-HAIRED POINTER

It is thought that this breed goes back at least to the seventeenth century, but that is a doubtful proposition. The German Stud Book of the Deutsch Kurzhaar was formed in 1872 when a dog called Hektor became No. 1 in Volume I; but the dog had without doubt been manufactured by using the English pointer as an important ingredient, and that breed had not been properly formed until the middle of the eighteenth century. Hunting conditions in Germany dictated a need for a dog of all-round ability. Game was scarce and therefore widespread, and it needed a dog with a big range to cover a lot of ground in the search. The game hunted varied too, ranging from rabbit and hare through partridge and pheasant, duck and geese to deer, and this meant that the dog was required to hunt, point, retrieve and track. It was, I suppose, the addition of the pursuit of deer to fur and feather that made normal pointers and

Learning to sit before handing over

seekers inadequate for the one-man hunter. The Germans took the dog which was to hand, a tracking bloodhound-like animal, still just extant, the Hanoverian Schweiss hound and, seeking speed and lightness, crossed it in the nineteenth century with the English pointer. From conformation and the popular liver and white ticking one might suspect that the French braque had something to do with the breeding, for the braque is a very old breed indeed. German short-haired pointers have been, from their beginnings, bred for work, and the result is a strong-bodied dog of considerable endurance. Whether it can encompass all the work credited to it may be a matter for debate, for to train one dog to be pointer, spaniel, retriever and deerhound according to the game present, or the terrain to be crossed, calls upon superlative skills in both dog and handler. Their task of hunting the wounded deer tended to produce hardmouth, but dogs worked solely on fur and feather for some generations are removing that failing from the breed.

German Short-Haired Pointer

CHARACTERISTICS The German short-haired pointer is a dual-purpose pointer-retriever, and this accounts for his excellence in the field, which requires a very keen nose, perseverance in searching, and enterprise. His style attracts attention; he is equally good on land and in water, is biddable, an extremely keen worker and very loyal.

GENERAL APPEARANCE A noble, steady dog showing power, endurance and speed, giving the immediate impression of an alert and energetic (not nervous) dog whose movements are well co-ordinated. Neither unduly small nor conspicuously large, but of medium size, and like the hunter, 'with a short back stands over plenty of ground'. Grace of outline, clean-cut head, sloping long

A German short-haired pointer bringing a duck from water

shoulders, deep chest, short back and powerful hindquarters, good bone composition, adequate muscle, well-carried tail and taut coat giving a thoroughbred appearance.

HEAD AND SKULL Clean-cut, neither too light nor too heavy, but well proportioned to the body. The skull sufficiently broad and slightly rounded. The furrow between the eyes not so deep, and the occiput not so pronounced as in the English pointer. The nasal bone rises gradually from nose to forehead (this is more pronounced in the male) and should never possess a definite stop as in the English pointer, but when viewed from the side there is a well-defined stop effect due to the position of the eyebrows. The lips fall away almost vertically from a somewhat protruding nose and continue in a slight curve to the corner of the mouth. Lips well developed but not overhung. Jaws powerful and sufficiently long to enable the dog to pick up and carry game. Dish-face and snipy muzzle are not desirable. Nose solid brown, wide nostrils well opened and soft.

EYES Medium size, soft and intelligent, not protruding nor too deep set. Varying in shades of brown to tone with coat. Light eye not desirable. Eyelids should close properly.

EARS Broad and set high; neither too fleshy nor too thin with a short soft coat; hung close to the head, no pronounced fold, rounded at the tip and should reach almost to the corner of the mouth when brought forward.

MOUTH Teeth sound and strong. Molar teeth meeting exactly and the eyeteeth should fit close in a true scissor bite. Neither overshot nor undershot.

NECK Moderately long, muscular and slightly arched, becoming larger towards the shoulders. Skin should not fit too closely.

FOREQUARTERS Shoulders sloping and very muscular with top of shoulder blades close; upper arm bones between shoulder and elbow long. Elbows well laid back, pointing neither outwards nor inwards. Forelegs straight and lean, sufficiently muscular and strong but not coarse-boned. Pasterns slightly sloping, almost straight but not quite.

BODY Chest must appear deep rather than wide but not out of proportion to the rest of the body; ribs deep and well sprung, never barrel-shaped nor flat as in the hound; back ribs reaching well down to tucked-up loins. Chest measurement immediately behind the elbows smaller than about a handsbreadth behind the elbows, so that the upper arm has freedom of movement. Firm, short back, not arched. The loin wide and slightly arched; the croup wide and sufficiently long, neither too heavy nor too sloping starting on a

Gordon setter: Winterwood Moon Beam

German short-haired pointer: Quintara Tyr

Hungarian Vizsla: Waidman Brok

Weimaraner: Fossana Bruno

German short-haired pointer on point

level with the back and sloping gradually towards the tail. Bones solid and strong, not clumsy and porous.

HINDQUARTERS The hips broad and wide falling slightly towards the tail. Thighs strong and well muscled. Stifles well bent. Hocks square with the body and slightly bent, turning neither in nor out. Pasterns nearly upright.

FEET Compact, close-knit, round to spoon-shaped, well padded, should turn neither in nor out. Toes well arched and heavily nailed.

TAIL Starts high and thick growing gradually thinner. Docked to medium length by two-fifths to half its length. When quiet tail should be carried down, and when moving horizontally, never held high over the back or bent.

COAT Skin should not fit loosely or fold. Coat short, flat and coarse to the touch, slightly longer under the tail.

COLOUR Solid liver, liver and white spotted, liver and white spotted and ticked, liver and white ticked, black and white.

WEIGHT AND SIZE Dogs 25–31·8 kg (55–70 lb), bitches 20·4–27·2 kg (45–60 lb). Size: dogs 58–64 cm (23–25 in) and bitches 53–59 cm (21–23 in) at the shoulder. Symmetry is most essential.

FAULTS Bone structure too clumsy, sway-back, head too large, deep wrinkles in forehead, cone-shaped skull or occiput too prominent. Ears too long or too closely set together, eyelids not closing properly. Wrinkles in neck. Feet or elbows turned inwards or outwards. Soft, sunken or splayed toes; cowhocks, straight hindlegs, or down on pasterns. Tail starting too low, undocked, too thick, curled up or too furry. Tri-coloured.

NOTE Male animals should have two apparently normal testicles fully descended into the scrotum.

THE HUNGARIAN VIZSLA

Hungary has stood through history on the path of great movements of people from east to west. People from Asia crossed the Carpathians, settled in Hungary and brought with them their dogs and the formation of the Magyar people. The Asians brought a yellow dog of mastiff type probably descended from the Asian wolf. The Magyars crossed it with their own old hound, the Pannonian. The progeny developed into a dog named after a small village in the Danube valley – Vizsla. The present dog of that name was evolved from this cross by introducing bloodhounds and pointers. The influence of the pointer is especially evident. The colour of the coat is an outstanding feature which has produced the breed's other name, the golden pointer. The Standard says that colour is russet gold, the lighter version of which is described by the Hungarians as 'crust of loaf of bread', and the solid yellow coat should, says the Standard, be 'short and straight, dense and coarse and feel greasy to the touch'.

The breed was produced to carry out the multitude of duties called for by the wide Hungarian plains. They were once used in packs to hunt boar and wolves, and they were much used to hunt up hares and forest deer. They were expected to point pheasants, partridge and woodcock on the plain and quail, geese and ducks from the marshes. They had to retrieve them all. Wars dividing Hungary and making her subservient to the Russians led to the breed falling into desuetude, but some got out to Austria, Italy, Czechoslovakia, America and from there to Britain. They are temperamental dogs not easy to train but affectionate and amusing: a charming, not much used, minority breed which could become a good retriever/pointer if anyone cared to work to make them so. But the competition from the German short-haired pointer and the Weimaraner is fierce.

Hungarian Vizsla

CHARACTERISTICS The Hungarian Vizsla should be lively and intelligent, obedient but sensitive, very affectionate and easily trained. It was bred for hunting for fur and feather on open ground or in thick cover, pointing and retrieving from both land and water.

GENERAL APPEARANCE A medium sized dog of distinguished appearance, robust and not too heavily boned.

HEAD AND SKULL The head should be gaunt and noble. The skull should be moderately wide between the ears with a median line down the forehead and a moderate stop. The muzzle should be a little longer than the skull and although tapering should be well squared at the end. The nostrils should be well developed, broad and wide. The jaws strong and powerful. The lips should cover the jaws completely and should be neither loose nor pendulous. The nose should be brown.

EYES Neither deep nor prominent, of medium size, being a shade darker in colour than the coat. The shape of the eyes should be slightly oval and the eyelids should fit tightly. A yellow or black eye is objectionable.

EARS The ears should be moderately low set, proportionately long with a thin skin, and hang down close to the cheeks; should be rounded 'V' shaped not fleshy.

MOUTH Sound white teeth meeting in a scissor bite; full dentition is desirable.

FOREQUARTERS Shoulders should be well laid and muscular, elbow straight pointing neither in nor out; the forearm should be long.

BODY Back should be level, short, well muscled, withers high. The chest should be moderately broad and deep with prominent breast bone. The distance from the withers to the lowest part of the chest should be equal to the distance from the chest to the ground. The ribs should be well sprung and the belly should be tight with a slight tuck-up beneath the loin. The croup should be well muscled.

HINDQUARTERS Should be straight when viewed from the ear, the thighs should be well developed with moderate angulation, the hocks well let down.

FEET Rounded with toes short, arched and well closed. A cat-like foot is desirable; hare foot is objectionable. Nails short, strong and a shade darker in colour than coat; dew claws should be removed.

GAIT Graceful and elegant with a lively trot and ground-covering gallop.

TAIL Should be of moderate thickness, rather low set, with one-third docked off. Whilst moving should be held horizontally.

COAT Should be short and straight, dense and coarse and feel greasy to the touch.

COLOUR Russet gold. Small white marks on chest and feet, though acceptable, are not desirable.

WEIGHT AND SIZE Optimum weight: 22–30 kg ($48\frac{1}{2}$–66 lb). Height at withers: dogs 57–64 cm ($22\frac{1}{2}$–25 in), bitches 53–60 cm (21–$23\frac{1}{2}$ in).

FAULTS Any departure from the foregoing points should be considered a fault, and the seriousness of the fault should be in exact proportion to its degree.

NOTE Male animals should have two apparently normal testicles fully descended into the scrotum.

THE WEIMARANER

This dog takes its name from the German town of Weimar. It was bred by the aristocracy of that state at the behest of the Grand Duke Karl of Saxe-Weimar-Eisenbach who ruled from 1775 to 1828. The Duke's wish was that by most careful – almost secret – breeding a superb hunting gundog should be produced. The breed's existence was formalised by the formation in 1897 of the Weimaraner Club of Germany by which time the colouration which gives the dog its name of Grey Ghost had been fixed. The most likely ancestor of the Weimaraner is the black St Hubert's Brachen bred by Benedictine monks from the ninth century. Black dogs constantly mated will in due course produce a grey pup. These pups bred together would produce a fixed colour of silver grey, mouse or roe grey, and those are the colours of the breed Standard today.

Coming as it does from bloodhound types the Weimaraner hunts with a low nose, like the old St Hubert, tracking wolves, deer, mountain lion and bear. It is thought that no pointer cross was used in the breeding, and the convex, rather than concave, nose and the ears bigger than those of the pointer are both perhaps reminiscent of the bloodhound. The Weimaraner is beautiful, and that beauty has led to its fall from grace as a gundog as the pet market has become the predominant influence. There is no doubt that it has the physique and background to be a dog that 'hunts, points and retrieves', but its mouth, descended from the deer hunter, is not always soft enough for the retrieving of small game. There are long-haired and wire-haired varieties, but the archetypal Grey Ghost has a smooth and splendid coat.

Weimaraner

CHARACTERISTICS In the case of the Weimaraner his hunting ability is the paramount concern, and any fault of body or mind which detracts from this ability should be penalised. The dog should display a temperament that is fearless, friendly, protective and obedient.

GENERAL APPEARANCE A medium sized grey dog with light eyes, he should present a picture of great driving power, stamina, alertness and balance. Above all, the dog should indicate ability to work hard in the field. Movement should be effortless and ground-covering and should indicate smooth co-ordination. When seen from the rear, the hind feet should parallel the front feet. When seen from the side, the top line should remain strong and level.

HEAD AND SKULL Moderately long and aristocratic, with moderate stop and slight median line extending back over the forehead. Rather prominent occipital bone and ears set well back. Measurement from the top of the nose to stop to equal that from the stop to the occipital prominence. The flews should be moderately deep, enclosing a powerful jaw. Foreface perfectly straight, delicate at the nostrils. Skin tightly drawn. Neck clean-cut and moderately long. Expression keen, kind and intelligent.

EYES Medium sized in shades of amber or blue grey, not protruding or too deep set, placed far enough apart to indicate good disposition and intelligence. When dilated under excitement the eyes may appear almost black.

EARS Long and lobular, slightly folded and set high. The ear when drawn alongside the jaw should end approximately one inch from the point of the nose.

MOUTH Well-set, strong and even teeth, well developed and proportionate to jaw with correct scissor bite (the upper protruding slightly over the lower teeth). Complete dentition is greatly desired. Grey nose, lips and gums of pinkish flesh shade.

FOREQUARTERS Forelegs straight and strong, with measurement from elbow to the ground equalling the distance from the elbow to the top of the withers.

BODY The length of the body from the highest point of the withers to the root of the tail should equal the measurement from the highest point of the withers to the ground. The top line should be level with a slightly sloping croup. The chest should be well developed and deep, shoulders well laid and snug. Ribs should be well sprung and long. Abdomen firmly held, moderately tucked up flank. The brisket should drop to the elbow.

HINDQUARTERS Moderately angulated with well-turned stifle. The hock joint well let down and turned neither in nor out. Musculation well developed.

FEET Firm and compact. Toes well arched, pads closed and thick. Nails short and grey or amber in colour. Dew claws allowable only on imported dogs.

TAIL Docked at a point such that the tail remaining shall just cover the scrotum in dogs and vulva in bitches. The thickness of the tail should be in proportion to the body and it should be carried in a manner expressing confidence and sound temperament. In the long-haired Weimaraner the tip of the tail should be removed.

COAT Short, smooth and sleek. In the long-haired Weimaraner the coat should be from one to two inches long on the body and somewhat longer on the neck, chest and belly. The tail and the backs of the limbs should be feathered.

COLOUR Preferably silver grey, shades of mouse or roe grey are admissible. The colour usually blends to a lighter shade on head and ears. A dark eel stripe frequently occurs along the back. The whole coat gives an appearance of metallic sheen. Small white marks allowable on chest but not on any other part of the body. White spots that have resulted from injuries should not be penalised. Colour of the long-haired Weimaraner as the short-haired.

SIZE Height at withers: dogs 61–69 cm (24–27 in), bitches 56–64 cm (22–25 in).

FAULTS Shyness or viciousness. Any colour or marking other than specified in this Standard.

NOTE Male animals should have two apparently normal testicles fully descended into the scrotum.

CHAPTER SIX

Training

If you intend to train your gundog to work with you in the field it is important that you buy a puppy bred from parents with a shooting lineage. This will most probably be shown by a pedigree full of field trial champions. A pedigree full of champions or show champions will indicate that the breeding is most unsuitable to produce a gundog and should be avoided at all costs. It is an unfortunate fact that most breeds of gundogs have split into two types, those bred for the show bench and those bred for work, and the two very rarely meet. So beware the show-bred litter.

Choosing a puppy is as hazardous as choosing a bride. Some experts say you should choose the boldest pup or that you should watch reactions to the noise of a hand-clap. Personally I think that once the right parentage has been selected the choice is in the lap of the gods. The best parentages produce great and poor pups, and which type you are going to get is a toss-up at twelve weeks when the choice is made. Most dogs can be made into good gundogs; those that are not are usually spoilt by their trainers. Having chosen your puppy from suitable parents, you should receive it at home at around twelve to fourteen weeks. It should be kennelled out of doors and will almost certainly howl for several nights at being deprived of its mother. You must just endure the agony and explain to angry neighbours that they must endure it too, but that it will be brief.

Puppy Training

Training starts pretty early in a puppy's life but training of such lightness that it is unaware that instruction is taking place. However hard you may want to try your expertise at training you must resist the temptation, and no formal training must take place at all until the puppy is around six months old. You must live with the paradox that the puppy must be trained, but that no formal training must be entered upon. You must however, from the beginning, say NO in disapproval of any misbehaviour, and NO will remain a big word in your handling vocabulary. NO, meaning desist at once from

A puppy should be played with and fondled

what you are doing, is used throughout a gundog's life, and it starts now. All properly bred, that is to say field trial bred, gundogs have wonderful natural attributes: supersonic hearing, a superb sense of smell, an instinct to retrieve and an interest to chase a moving object. So you will not have to teach your puppy to use its eyes to mark the fall of a bird, use its nose to follow game, or use its instinct to retrieve. You will, however, have to transform its instinct to chase into a discipline to sit when something runs or falls. That is the essence of all training, and everything you do will be directed towards that end. This fact cannot be over emphasised, for learning to sit when all its instincts scream for a chase is the big lesson that a gundog has to be taught. As a famous trainer once said, 'A dog you can stop is a made dog.' All trainers should remember that always. *A gundog must be trained to sit when it wants to chase.*

At first your new puppy must be allowed to settle at home and get used to its new surroundings and to you. You, who are going to train it and become therefore its pack leader, must start to build up a relationship with it by handling it, talking to it and feeding it. Dogs have a pack instinct, part of which is a sense of pack leadership, and you, the trainer, are going, in the dog's mind, to become that ever-obeyed pack leader. To this purpose you should always feed your dog yourself.

For the next six months you are going to educate your puppy without its realising what is going on, so that at the end of that time training of a serious kind can start. At six months the puppy should do the following:

1. Come when called by name and maybe when whistled.
2. Sit to the command SIT, hand signal and whistle.
3. Lie down, in a place indicated, to the command BED.
4. Get into the car to the command GET IN.
5. Spend a penny to the command BUSY.
6. Walk to heel to the command HEEL on and off the lead most of the time.
7. Wait to the command WAIT while the trainer walks away a little.
8. Jump a two-foot jump to the command OVER.
9. Enter water on the command GET IN and swim and splash around happily.
10. Stop doing whatever it is doing to the command NO.

Please note that it is not then expected to retrieve and *no retrieving training should have taken place at all.*

Note also that nothing resembling a training session must take place. Each lesson must last not more than a minute or so, each situation must be simple, and no admonition must be administered, for the puppy is a baby.

When the puppy has settled into its new surroundings and is being played with and fondled to start the build up of the special relationship between it and its trainer, it should be brought into the house from time to time, for every dog must be house-trained.

Bed

In the house there should be a place for it to stay, just one place, a basket or a rug in a corner, and it should be placed there with the command BED. The puppy will not stay in place but should be put back gently with the command BED. This is no time to look for obedience: it is the mere repetition that is of importance now. Remember that the puppy has only the intelligence of a baby and can learn and retain nothing. But from time to time the puppy will sleep in its corner and gradually get used to being there.

Busy

Pennies will almost certainly be spent on precious carpets, and house training must start. This is achieved by putting the puppy out at very frequent intervals, and as it spends a penny you should say BUSY. This of course means nothing to the puppy, but one day when the puppy is running around you will say BUSY and to your amazement it will spend a penny to command. It is important that it should do so before you set out on a journey or before it spends a night in a hotel, but remember that this lesson is learnt by constant repetition and not by disciplining.

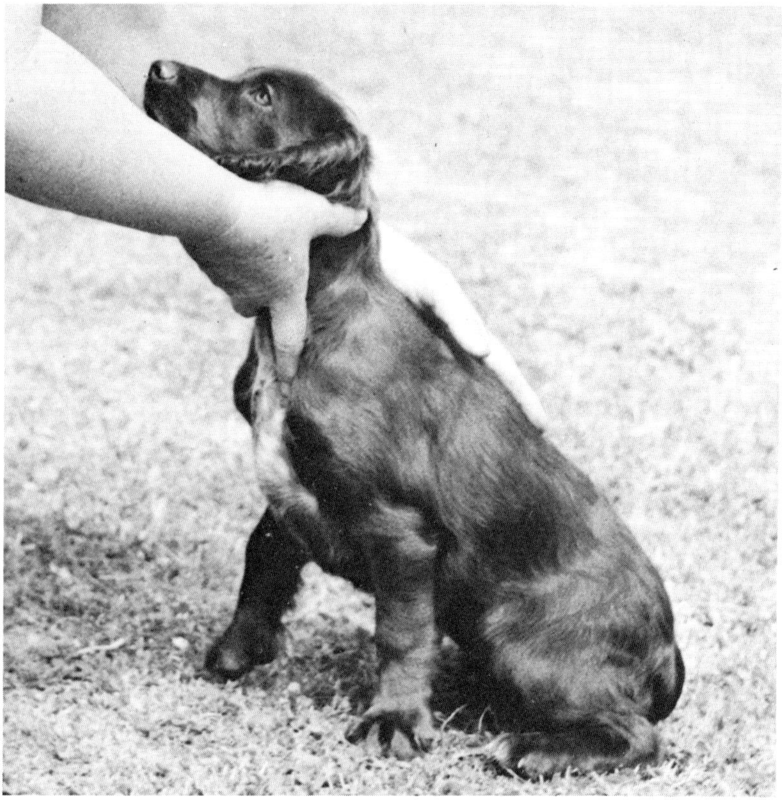

A cocker spaniel puppy receiving its first lesson in sitting

Sit

You should teach your puppy to sit by pushing its behind to the ground with one hand whilst the other hand holds its chest, and as you push it down you should say SIT. This you should do fairly frequently just holding the puppy in the sit position for a few seconds each time. Soon you will find that the puppy will sit when it hears the command SIT, and then you should hold up your hand with the palm facing the dog every time you say SIT. In due course the puppy will sit at the sight of your up-raised hand. None of this must be forced on the puppy. All that is necessary is gentle repetition from time to time. No prolonged lesson must be entered into, and no scolding must be administered if the order is not obeyed.

Wait

Your puppy will have several meals a day. It should be taught to wait by its food bowl. Place the bowl on the ground and bring the puppy within a few yards of it; for a second or two before it rushes to its food bowl, restrain it with both hands, and as it wriggles say WAIT. Do this every mealtime, and before long the puppy will automatically wait before it feeds. This is an important lesson, for it is teaching the puppy restraint in an exciting situation, and this is the foundation on which will be built your puppy's discipline to stop and watch a started hare, or an escaping pheasant, depart.

It is also the base from which to teach a dog to respond to hand signals which is something it is going to have to do perfectly as a working gundog as you direct it to find a piece of game the fall of which has not been seen. To carry out an unseen retrieve your dog must change directions as indicated by a wave of your arm. This is an essential piece of drill, and now quietly and without realising that it is being taught your puppy will start to learn it.

Go Right, Go Left, Get Out

Once your puppy will sit at wait before its food bowl you set it on its way by a wave of your arm in the direction of the bowl. These arm movements are important and will be used always from now on. They must be plain and positive. The hand must be held upright above your head and swept down through 180 degrees. You should also step in the direction in which you move the arm so that the dog sees an obvious direction signal. This is all you do. You place your dog to the right of the bowl full of food, and with your left hand you wave it off on its way, stepping to the left as you do so.

Puppies hate the lead at first . . .

. . . but get used to it . . .

. . . pretty quickly

Next time you place the dog on the left of the bowl and wave it right with your right arm. Then you place the dog in front of its bowl and with a wave of your hand thrown forward with palm open you say GET OUT. In future you will get your dog out straight ahead of you perhaps across rivers and obstacles by giving this command of GET OUT accompanied by the thrusting forward wave of your open palm. Now it is learning to do it without realising that any teaching is taking place.

Heel

When it is a few months old you will want to start taking your dog for walks and for a run around a field, and for this purpose you will need to have the dog on a lead. The best sort of lead is a slip lead which can be made easily from a piece of cord. This type of lead is useful for teaching a dog to walk to heel because if it is put on properly it will tighten when it is pulled as you tug the dog back to heel and loosen when released. The right way to put on a lead is with the lead coming across the top of the dog's neck into your hand. It should here be noted that a gundog should never wear a collar when working. It can catch up on a branch or fence and asphyxiate the dog or catch on an underwater snag and drown it. A gundog should always work with its neck unencumbered. To start with just place a lead on your dog and let it wriggle and play with it. It will certainly do this, for it will object to having something stuck round its neck and will try to run away from it and shake it off. Just leave it to do this and make no attempt to pick up the lead and after a time or two the puppy will run around happily dragging the lead behind it.

When the puppy is accustomed to wearing the lead pick it up

An early lesson in walking to heel for a Labrador puppy

with your left hand and pull the dog towards your left heel and say HEEL. Say also SSST. This hissing command is most valuable. It is used forever to bring the dog to HEEL, to attract its attention and to stop it moving from sit. It is very useful and, importantly, it is almost silent. A dog is trained to walk on the left of a right-handed shot and on the right of a left-handed shot. It will take a time or two to get used to having you on the end of the lead, and it will also pull ahead and sideways and stay back behind too. As it does so you pull it to your side saying each time HEEL and remembering that having pulled the slip lead tight round the dog's neck you must release the pressure at once for you must not choke your dog in this lesson. It may take quite some time to get your dog to walk quietly by your side on the lead, so do not rush it and do not force the dog. Take your time: be persistent in pulling the dog to heel and patient in waiting for the lesson to sink in. The lessons should last no longer than a minute, after which the lead is taken off and the dog left to run around.

Come To Me

From the moment you get to know your puppy you should call it by its name which should be monosyllabic. A single syllable name is

SIT : teaching a puppy to wait while the handler retreats

to be preferred because it is easy to shout decisively, and it should be a name easily distinguished from the commands of BED, BUSY, SIT, WAIT, GET OUT, GET OVER, GET IN, HIE LOST, HEEL and NO which will be the only words used by you to control your dog. You should call your dog's name and squat down with open arms patting the ground and repeating the name in an exciting and pleasurable way. When the dog comes bounding in it should be stroked and fondled and have a great fuss made of it. When the puppy always comes rushing to you when called you should blow three blasts on the whistle. From now on you should always blow three blasts when you call your puppy, so that in due course it will respond to the whistle call alone. But you must not chastise the puppy for failing to respond; you should just keep on calling and whistling and making a fuss. The puppy will get the message in time. If the puppy shows reluctance to come, run away calling its name and it will soon follow, especially if you hide out of sight.

WAIT, WAIT, WAIT.

Wait

By now the puppy will sit when you raise your hand, and you should start to try to leave it sitting whilst you move away. The object of this exercise is to enable you, when the dog is mature, to leave it in one spot whilst you go off on your affairs and disappear. You should be able to leave the dog sitting for very long periods, but at this time all you need to achieve is that you should be able to back away a few yards leaving the puppy sitting. You should sit the dog and move backwards slowly whilst holding your hand up saying WAIT, WAIT, WAIT. The dog will amost certainly set out to follow you, and here you start something you must always remember: go and replace the puppy on the spot from which it has moved. Every time from now on you must go back to the puppy and replace it on the spot. However far you have moved away, even if it is a hundred yards or more, *you must go back to the puppy and replace it on the exact spot.* There is no need to get upset if the dog repeatedly moves forward. Just rely on constant repetition; one day the message will click, and you will be able to disappear and leave the dog sitting exactly where you left it for several minutes.

A puppy learning to heel on a lead

Jump – Get Over

When the puppy is coming up to six months of age, erect a small jump about 18 inches high in a position from which it cannot be circumnavigated and cross it yourself, calling the puppy to you and saying OVER, OVER, OVER. When it comes across frequently, send it over the jump with a wave of your hand shouting OVER, OVER. Soon the puppy will leap backwards and forwards to command.

Heel off Lead

At around six months you can start to teach your puppy to walk to heel off the lead. Start by walking the puppy to heel on the lead and then drop the lead so that it trails on the floor. After a time or two take off the lead. Soon the dog will realise that it has a new-found freedom and will start to wander away. You must pat your left thigh and call HEEL, HEEL. Your earlier command of HEEL when pulling the dog to heel on a lead should bring it immediately back to your side, but if this is not so further drill on the lead is indicated when you must insist by use of the check cord that the dog stays strictly at heel with its head just in advance of your left knee.

A puppy walking to heel off the lead

Wondering whether to go in . . .

Water Work

All gundogs will be required to enter or cross water to retrieve game, so an early introduction to water is necessary. Generally speaking most breeds of gundog love water and can be restrained only with difficulty from plunging in. This is not always the case, however: some dogs are most reluctant to get into water on first acquaintance and remain so all their lives, but these are happily exceptions. So you must find water for your puppy to try. It should be ideally a still, shallow pond or a slow flowing river with gently sloping sides. A very precipitous bank must be avoided as must a very fast current for both will frighten a puppy. Just take your puppy to this shallow water and walk in yourself in gumboots. Call the puppy to you encouragingly by name and with some reluctance and with much slapping of the water with its paw the puppy will dash in and out of the water. There is no need to attempt much more at these early stages which are merely opportunities for a puppy to become accustomed to a new and slightly frightening medium. In due course if you are patient in letting the dog get used to water at its own pace it will swim a little and then you are on your way. Never try to hurry this process, never push or pull the puppy in and never

. . . All right so far . . .

. . . It's not so bad if your boss comes in too

throw a puppy in. If it is very reluctant a bit of biscuit should be thrown in and the puppy invited to go and get it. Greed will often start the entry into water and as the biscuit is thrown further and further out so will the puppy get better.

This elementary water work is an important piece of learning. It should not be hurried, should take place preferably in warm weather, should be accomplished in frequent short sessions and must involve no force, ever.

Traffic

You must never take your puppy on a road without its being on a lead. Even when it is a most experienced dog and you merely cross a road whilst out shooting the lead must always be put on until you are back in a field again. This is because vehicles may be rushing past when a dog shies away from another dog or from any sudden noise with fatal results to the dog and maybe even to human beings. It is inexcusable for a dog to be the cause of an accident. So your puppy must be exposed to traffic and people and when walking steadily to heel on a lead should be taken out on main roads and into populous places. At first it will shy away from booming lorries and screaming motor bikes and as it does you should pull it into heel and stroke it soothingly. It will also sniff at people, their baskets and their dogs. It is good training to expose a dog to these distractions; you must pull the dog to heel every time it veers off to inspect something new and say HEEL at each pull of the lead.

Get in a Car

Your dog must be prepared to travel everywhere in a car or a wagon and must get into them on the command GET IN. A car or station wagon is too high off the ground for a young puppy to jump in, so it must be placed in it to start with. As you lift the dog into place, say GET IN. Always do this, and when it is big enough to jump in it should leap into the car when you give the command. Some puppies are shy of getting into a car and some are car-sick when travelling. To overcome shyness the dog should be fed in the car. If its food bowl is placed in the car the dog will certainly leap in after it and so will associate the car with the pleasurable act of eating and gradually overcome its fear. Dogs often grow out of car-sickness but for those that do not there are two courses open. One is to give it some form of tranquilliser before setting out on a journey, and the other is to fill the dog's place with newspaper and when it is sick stop, roll-up the newspaper, dispose of it and drive on. I use this newspaper method, and the dog seems to arrive none the worse for wear at the end of the journey.

Formal Training

So we come to six months with, we hope, much accomplished with no mishap and no strain on puppy or trainer. What we should have is a happy puppy more or less under control coming to us at the call of his name and three whistle blasts, walking more or less peaceably at heel, jumping a little jump to command, sitting to a raised hand on one whistle blast, ready to walk on its lead among people and traffic and getting into its bed or a car and spending a penny on command and waiting when told to whilst we move away some distance. Now we can set about formal training. Not, be it noted, if the puppy does not do all these things properly. If most of this initial training needs to be learned everything must wait until these basics are well and invariably performed, because if you start to build on weak foundations all future training will collapse around your ears.

Equipment

We need some equipment for this formal training, but not much. We have already a slip lead and a whistle. I think that the old

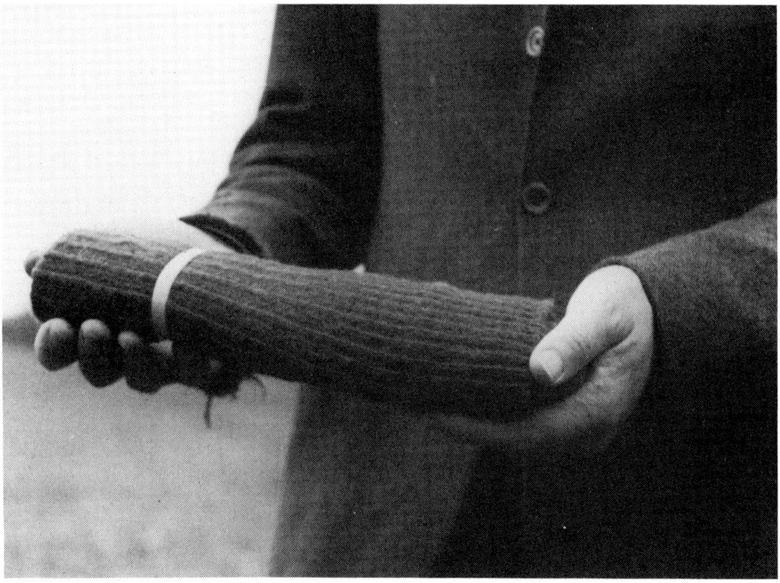

Dummy covered in a sock

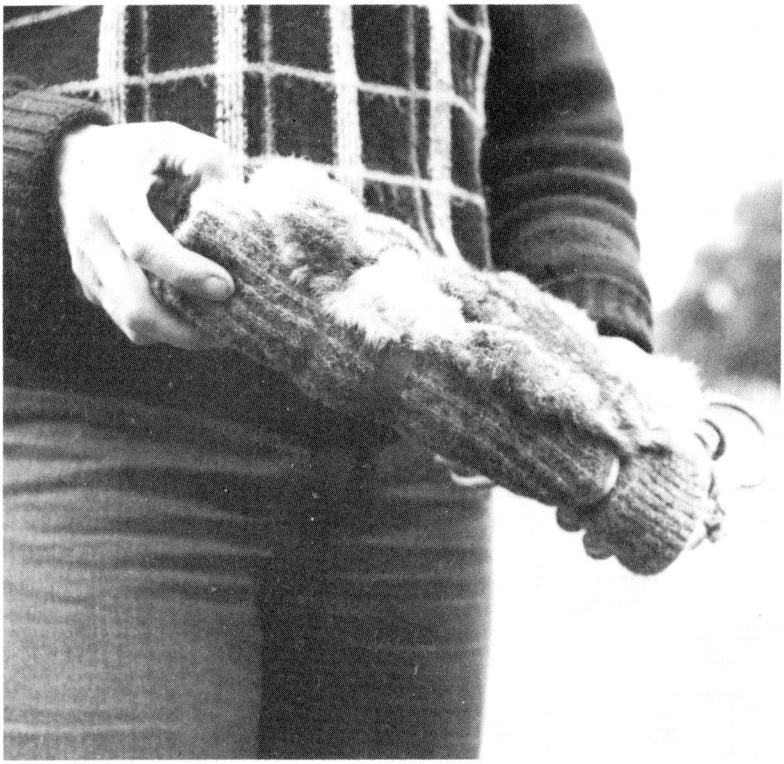

Dummy covered in fur

fashioned pea-whistle is best because it can be heard in difficult conditions, and unlike the other possibilities of a silent whistle or a horn whistle it does not so easily get bunged up with bits of straw or fluff. In addition we need a collection of dummies. They can be made from sacking or canvas and should be about 18 inches long and stuffed with rags, straw, stones and wood to weigh $1-1\frac{1}{2}$ lb. One should be made of rabbit skin, and one should be filled with corks or foam rubber so that it floats. All these can be bought with rope handles with a toggle on to help throwing. We are going to accustom the dog to the sound of gunfire and we are going to want to get dummies over rivers and hedges, and both these requirements can be met by buying a dummy launcher which works on .22 blanks and will lift a dummy fifty yards in the air.

Now a structured programme of training must be started and carried out without a break for several months and with repeated regularity. The old days of learning quietly during the ordinary round of life are ending, and the puppy will know that it is under instruction and must learn to obey the orders given.

Seen Retrieves

All this instruction must be carried out in a solitary manner. No other people or dogs must ever be present to cause a distraction. First we must start retrieving, and here a lesson must be learnt by the trainer. This is important and only overlooked at the peril of all future progress, but it is simple: *the dog must be made to sit and wait every time a dummy is thrown.* This is vital teaching, for remember that the lynch pin of training is that the dog's instinct to chase must be transformed into the discipline of stopping when something falls or runs or rolls. One day the dog is going to be asked to walk to heel in line through roots or across stubble seeing bird after bird shot to fall all around, and it will have to sit to each shot and fall, with no attempt to run-in or chase. The worst sort of dog in the field is the one that runs-in. It is a menace to itself, its handlers and everyone else concerned with the day's sport, and these horrors are manu-

Spaniel sitting to a thrown dummy while restrained by lead

SIT before retrieving in the rabbit pen

factured at this moment in their training. They are not taught to sit and wait when they first come to learn retrieving.

Sit your dog, throw a dummy high in the air, tell the dog to sit, wait a full 30 seconds and then with a wave of the hand give the command HIE LOST. The puppy is used to following your hand signals because of the food-bowl training you have given it, and it should go out at once for the dummy. As it picks up blow three blasts on the whistle, and the dog should come running straight back. If it does, take the dummy gently from it and make a great fuss of the dog. As you take the dummy from the dog say DROP or DEAD. I

SIT while the dummy is thrown

always say DROP, and from this start the dog learns to release what is in its mouth to the word DROP. This you will want it to do when it is mature and holding something unsuitable in its mouth, and the training starts now. If it hesitates to go out walk forward with it, gesturing towards the dummy and the moment it picks it up turn and run away whilst whistling the recall signal. Usually the puppy carries out this first retrieve perfectly, but it may refuse to pick up or mouth the dummy. The remedy is to abandon the lesson and give the puppy the dummy to play with: put it in its mouth and have it walk around carrying it at heel. Soon the puppy will enjoy carrying the dummy. When the dog brings the dummy properly to hand you should say SIT before it hands over. This delivery attitude is ideal because the dog's head is up and game can be removed easily. Some trainers regard this lesson as fussy. I think it provides a firm discipline at the moment of hand-over and stops the dog jumping up.

Once a simple seen retrieve can be achieved without difficulty you should throw the dummy, sit the dog, and then turn and call it to heel and walk away. Go about 30 yards away and send the dog, after sitting it, for the dummy. From now on every seen retrieve

Handler running away to encourage a pup to come smartly to him

A German short-haired pointer coming in with a dummy as the trainer gives the SIT *signal. Note that the spectators are steady*

The German short-haired pointer sits to hand over

should be of this walk-on and go-back sort so that the distance gets up to 100 yards. This way the dog gets a lot of exercise and starts to develop its memory. The final stage of this get-back retrieve is when on the way away from the dummy you stop the dog at sit and walk on yourself, say, 10 yards. Then face the dog, raise your arm above your head with palm facing forward and, sweeping your arm forward and down, give the command GET OUT. The dog should respond because of your food-bowl training, and henceforth this is how you should carry out this retrieve. In time the distance between the dog and the dummy can be 100 yards and from you to the dog, say, 50 yards.

You must not, now that you have a dog that can retrieve, over-indulge the pleasure. Very few seen retrieves should be given, say two per training session; and training sessions should be not more than 10 minutes duration, and if possible there should be two or three sessions a day. From now on short and sweet must be your watchword. You must not prolong training sessions, must not repeat a lesson too frequently and must end a session, if things start going wrong, by stopping the misunderstood lesson and giving the dog something simple to do that it will accomplish successfully before you return home.

Unseen Retrieves

The food bowl should be used to prepare the dog for unseen retrieves. Hide the bowl and signal the dog towards it with the wave of an arm and the command HIE LOST. The smell of food will be strong in its nostrils, and so there should be no question of its not setting off and hunting fast for the hidden bowl. Do this several times at feeding time, and then you should be ready to attempt an unseen retrieve with the dummy.

Put the dummy hidden in light cover and bring the dog out to sit about 10 yards away and downwind so that the scent comes strongly to it. Wave your arm, command HIE LOST and the retrieve should be accomplished without problem. If there is some hesitation walk the dog forward to find the dummy and then walk back to the starting point again to repeat the lesson.

Several lessons can be started whilst this retrieving progress is under way, for it is a programme of increasing complexity and it should be varied with other work.

At this stage, stopping to one whistle blast on the way out and on the return should be worked on, and getting into cover and more advanced water work undertaken.

Stop on Way Out and Back

When the dog is walking at heel you should blow one whistle blast, stop and say SIT. This should be repeated several times per training session, and no further stopping work should be attempted until this lesson is very firmly embedded. So drilled-in must it become that the act of your stopping produces a sit from the dog. When this is so, and not before, you can try controlling the dog when it is running free. Set the dog off from heel and when it is 10 yards away blow the whistle, say SIT and hold up your hand. If the dog stops, good; if it stops and sits, very good indeed. If it takes no notice, run forward, blow your whistle and push the dog down whilst saying SIT.

The dog should soon learn the lesson; if it is sticky and refuses to respond it should go back on the lead, but this time a very long thin cord known as a check-cord. Let it wear the cord and get used to dragging it around; then when it is running around blow the whistle, shout SIT and raise your hand. If the dog takes no notice pull on the check cord and repeat the commands. The dog should soon learn to sit and, when it does, try again without the check-cord; if you are successful the stopping lessons can go forward again.

The object is that when the dog is going in any direction it should stop at one whistle blast. The reason for this is firstly so that in future if the dog is beginning to chase it can be stopped in its tracks, and secondly so that when it is hunting for a dummy or a bird and needs to be directed it will stop to one whistle blast, look back at the handler and take a hand signal to move in another direction.

A dog should always be whistled to sit before a new direction signal is given. One of those directions is to come towards the handler, and so you must introduce the lesson 'stop-on-your-way-back-to-me'. This requires that the dog will stay at sit while the trainer walks away. We started this lesson during initial training. Now it must be extended and perfected. You should sit the dog and walk backwards with your hand held up whilst saying WAIT, WAIT, WAIT. Do short distances at first and gradually extend them. The object is to be able to walk away and disappear for 60 seconds, then emerge and walk back to the dog. This is an important point: *always walk back to the dog* and make a fuss of it when you have completed a wait lesson. This is so that the dog gets to realise that it must stay where it has been sat and not move. The chances are that the puppy will crawl forward on its belly or even run forward towards the trainer. If it does so the trainer must always take the dog back to the spot at which it was sat and start the lesson again. *The dog must be replaced on the spot every time it moves.*

This lesson may take a very long time to be absorbed and is the cause of much misunderstanding and bad temper; but it must be persisted in with great patience and with absolutely no loss of temper and no punishment. Persistence will ensure that the dog will get the message. Once it does it should be sat at WAIT at every training session and when the trainer crosses an obstacle. This is important because in the field there are few things more infurating than a dog that dashes ahead of its owner to cross the next stile knocking over an unfortunate gun precariously balanced on top. Nor should a dog enter a new field or covert ahead of its owner. It should wait while the owner crosses the obstacle, jump across when called up and come straight to heel.

This waiting discipline must be established extremely firmly in the dog before it is called up by the three blasts of the recall signal. When it is thought safe to do this call it up and as it is on its way back to you blow the stop blast, raise your hand and shout WAIT. The dog will almost certainly keep charging on towards you and you should whistle and give the command WAIT time and again as it approaches. It probably will not stop until it is next to you. There is no answer to this except constant repetition. The distance of the call-up should be very short to start with, and gradually the dog will stop a longer and longer distance away from you.

This is an important and basic lesson which may take many months to master, but work on it must be carried out throughout the basic training period until it is perfectly carried out every time.

Enter Cover

Gradually the dog should be introduced to cover. A trained dog must enter the most impenetrable cover on command, but at this stage we just want the dog to get into cover to retrieve a dummy or to hunt up for game. You should start with light cover no thicker than long grass by giving the dog an unseen retrieve to do. Once it will hunt around in long grass the dummy should be placed in thicker cover like bracken and when movement in bracken is uninhibited the dummy should be placed in brambles. The puppy will almost certainly walk around the bramble patch hesitating before pushing in and you should encourage its entry by calling GET IN, GET IN and giving the pushing GET OUT hand signal.

Some dogs are very shy of thick cover and may need the encouragement of being offered a biscuit to pursue into the brambles.

They can practically never resist the smell of food and will usually make a most hesitant and tip-toed entry in search of a biscuit thrown deeper and deeper into the cover until they are pushing forward and under the thickest of the thick. When this happy event occurs you can replace the biscuit with the dummy, and with luck the dog will hunt for a dummy in thick covert from now on. It will certainly have to do so to root out a tucked-in hen-pheasant, and this is the time when it first learns to do this. You should not try to get your puppy into nettles. Their tender extremities react painfully to them and you will find that an older tougher dog takes nettles in its stride whereas a puppy can be put off cover of any sort for a long time by being forced into nettles.

Advanced Water Work

Now the dog should be introduced to retrieving from on and over water. Go to your usual calm water, sit the dog on the bank and throw the dummy in a little way. After a pause, give the command

A spaniel swimming strongly for a dummy

A Labrador demonstrates one way of entering the water

HIE LOST and when it gets to the water's edge say GET IN, GET IN. The dog should enter the water, swim out to the dummy, pick it, swim back and hand over. If the dog refuses to enter the water your puppy training has proved inadequate; the dummy should be thrown just a foot or two from the bank and the dog sent straight away. If the entry is shallow it should be able to walk in and collect the dummy; if it does you can very slowly increase the distance the dummy is thrown. If this does not work you must go back to tempting the dog in with biscuits until it will swim quite strongly. The dog may get into the water, collect the dummy and then drop it the moment it leaves the water in order to shake itself. This fault must be overcome because in the field it could be unfortunate if the dog were to collect a runner and drop it on leaving the water. One great

A young Labrador retrieving a dummy from water

expert asserts that no sensible dog would drop a runner and so he would not downgrade a dog in a field trial for this fault; but it is a fault and a potentially dangerous one so it must be overcome. To try to do this you should rush away from the bank calling the dog which should run after you so that you can take the retrieve as it comes alongside. As a dog attempts to drop the dummy you should say NO, NO, NO to impress upon it the necessity of holding on to the dummy.

When retrieving a dummy thrown on to the water is carried out properly the dummy should be thrown across the river on to the opposite bank in full view of the dog which should then be sent across. There is normally no problem with this retrieve, and the progress from it is to put the dummy a long way out from the far bank and get the dog over and out to the retrieve. To get the dummy away from the bank you need a dummy launcher or a tennis racket and ball or an assistant on the far bank. Across-river retrieves from now on must all be made from inland so that the puppy does not get used to hunting the bank the moment it leaves the water.

The next refinement of water work is that the start of the retrieve should be from well back from the bank. In working tests and field trials the start is always from a long way back to show that the dog will enter water of its own accord without the handler standing over it and putting pressure on it to cross. You should send your dog for its retrieves from 10 to 20 yards back from the bank; when it approaches the water, perhaps down the bank and out of your sight, you should shout GET OVER, GET OVER and with luck it will enter the water and swim across. If it starts rushing around on the near bank you must move forward and by voice and hand signal force it over. You must continue until movement into the water from close quarters is carried out every time and then start to move back again from the bank.

Getting Used to Gunfire

During its early months a puppy should be introduced to noise by having hands clapped, boards banged together, tin cans beaten and, if you live in the country, a starting pistol fired over it whilst it is at its food bowl. The purpose of all this noise-making at this time is to connect noise with the pleasurable action of eating and thereby to try to avoid its being gun-shy. In the field the dog will of course be bombarded with the discharge of twelve bores in great fusillades during a big drive and it must take no more notice of it than do the human beings causing the din. During the formal training phase a

German short-haired pointers sit to the firing of a dummy launcher

conscious effort must be made to get the dog used to gunfire: the method is simple but needs to be carried out correctly so that problems are not created. On a farm or in a kennels there can be guns banging all around so that the chances are the puppies growing up will get accustomed to distant gunfire; but, for a dog trained at home, introduction to it can be a sudden transition. *No gun may be fired over a dog until it has grown accustomed to distant gunfire.*

To introduce your puppy to gunfire you need an assistant armed with a shotgun or a shotgun with an Ackvoke adaptor for firing .22 blanks, or a starting pistol or a dummy launcher. You should send the assistant 100 yards away to fire a shot. Have the dog at your side and when the shot is fired say SIT and make a fuss of your dog. If all goes well have the helper move up to 50 yards and fire another shot while you carry out the same procedure. If this goes well stop the lesson for the day. From now on you should always give the command SIT when a gun is fired for this is one of the moments when a dog must sit. It is important that this lesson is absolutely certainly absorbed because in the field the discharge of a gun will result in a bird falling from the air, or a hare skidding to a halt or worse still a bird falling and dashing for cover or a hare or rabbit wounded and legging it across country. These are moments when the dog's instinct is to chase and when that instinct must be modified by training into the discipline to stop. *A dog must be taught* always *to sit when a gun is fired.*

From now on the shots are fired closer and closer to the dog until at last it is fired by you with the dog sitting beside you. Once you can do this you can be sure that your dog is not gun-shy – a terrible disease – or gun-nervous – a curable complaint. If the puppy is gun-shy, which may be an hereditary complaint, it may turn out to be incurable in which case you must abandon all hope of training a good gundog and maybe talk to the breeder about his taking it back and refunding your money or exchanging it. On the other hand it may be just displaying a bad case of gun-nervousness which many dogs destined to be great performers in the field can show on first meeting gunfire. This shows itself by the dog flinching and turning its head or backing away whenever a gun is fired. This can be overcome by careful nursing by keeping the gunfire at a distance for a long time; bring it closer very gradually and, as well as your command SIT, make a great fuss of the dog, giving it a titbit of biscuit or meat, so that gunfire becomes associated with a pleasant occasion. This should do the trick.

Once the dog is steady to gunfire you should train it to sit at the raising of the gun. This is good discipline which reinforces the vital action of sitting when a gun is fired and is intended to ensure that when you are out shooting your dog's discipline is to sit whenever shooting takes place. Apart from the very serious reason for this drill it is also, when well learnt, an assurance that at the expense of one cartridge you can stop your dog if it is tempted to run-in.

Drop to Moving Things

Throughout its training period a dog must have lessons in sitting when something moves. Already you will have made your dog sit whenever a dummy is thrown. *It cannot be too often repeated that a dog must have drummed into it that as an object falls it must sit.*

Now the lesson can be extended by making the dog sit whilst things are rolled around it. These things can be balls or Richard Sharpe's slices of log (Richard Sharpe was the inventor of dummy training) or even the launcher dummy fired along the ground to bounce and roll away. At first, roll the object when the dog is on its lead, blow the whistle once, jerk the lead and say SIT. Before too long the dog will sit as the object bounces away. Now roll the thing past the dog when it is running free off the lead. As it sees it and sets off towards it – as it almost certainly will – blow the whistle, raise your hand palm outwards and say SIT. Throw things around the dog frequently and carry out the stopping drill: the dog should start to sit the moment it sees the rolling object.

You should now station an assistant hidden behind a hedge, building or other screen and when the dog is running free the rolling thing must be thrown across its path. The surprise advent of something bouncing away may well start a run-in, however steady the dog has been up to now, and you will need to be very quick and firm with your whistle-hand-and-SIT stop drill.

Of course dogs frequently fail to respond to this stopping drill, and no progress towards perfection can be made whilst a dog has a propensity to run-in to these rolling objects; it will certainly run-in in the field or in a field trial or a working test, and a dog which runs-in in competition is promptly eliminated – and quite rightly so. A dog which runs-in is the great menace of the shooting field. So if your dog is a runner-in during this training stage you must revert to the check-cord. This is a long, say 20 yard, cord on which the dog will, in theory, rush forward, so that you will be able to grab the cord and pull the dog up short in its headlong progress. At the same time you blow one whistle blast and shout SIT. After being pulled up short every time it runs-in the dog should learn to stop when something rolls past. Then you can remove the check-cord and try the lesson on the unfettered dog. A sensitive, intelligent dog will have learned the lesson: it will sit when the moving object flashes past and all will be well from then on. Unfortunately not all dogs are so accommodating: many dogs know whether they are on or off the check-cord and are steady when on and wild when off. That is why I said earlier that 'in theory' the dog would enable you to check its progress. In theory the check-cord works, but whilst suggesting its use I must say that I think a potentially good dog does not need it whilst a bad dog is always bad when off it.

From now on you are ready for training the dog to be steady to the real thing. Unfortunately steadiness to running pheasants or partridges is something that the amateur dog trainer can only prove on a shooting day when it is to be hoped that all the earlier steady-to-dummy-and-to-rolling-objects lessons will pay off and ensure that the dog sits as the bird disappears. Further training can however take place to ensure steadiness to ground game. This training involves a tame rabbit on the lawn or, if it can be found with a local gamekeeper or dog trainer, in a rabbit pen. I have steadied many dogs to ground game using a big old tame rabbit on the lawn and I advise its use to one-dog trainers. The drill is simple. The rabbit is removed from its hutch and put on the lawn, and the dog is brought along on its lead. Every time the rabbit moves the lead is jerked and the stop whistle blown. The dog should be called up to the rabbit which is encouraged to move with the help of the trainer's toe and at every movement of the rabbit the stop drill must be enacted. When the dog stops at every movement of the rabbit it should be brought to the lawn off the lead and the previous actions performed. The dog should drop to the rabbit's movement. If it does not it must go on to the check-cord with a view to stopping its chase before it is left off the lead again.

The use of the rabbit pen is similar though the action is more hectic. The rabbits are wild, hiding under natural or artificial cover,

A Hungarian Viszla on point in the rabbit pen

and they should rush around all over the place so that the puppy is tremendously tempted and you, the trainer, have many opportunities to exercise the restraining drill. Whether you are confined to a lawn rabbit or have the excitement of the rabbit pen you must, when the puppy sits to rabbit movement, enter upon the slightly hair-raising task of having the dog retrieve a dummy whilst the rabbits are running around. The rabbit must be on the lawn or 'in situ' in the rabbit pen. The dummy is thrown near to the rabbit and the dog sent for the dummy. With luck the rabbit will move whilst the retrieve is in progress, and you will know whether your training has paid off. If the dog goes to the dummy and ignores the rabbit you are home and dry. If it veers off towards the rabbit blow hard on the whistle and shout SIT. If it stops you are on the way to success. If it rushes after the rabbit you still have problems to solve and must go back to the check-cord again. If after much effort the dog remains a chaser you must reluctantly give up all idea of its becoming a useful companion in the field.

Change Direction

You have got to be able to stop your dog and move it in any direction required by you. It should go left, right, out or back exactly as you require. If you have been using my method the dog will already take hand signals on its way to its food bowl to go and get its food to the right, left, or out. Now you must procure transition from that accomplishment to the retrieving of dummies. I use a clock face to teach this lesson. Sit your dog in the centre of the clock. Throw a dummy to three o'clock. Walk to six o'clock. Turn and face the dog. Hold your hand above your head, move it to the right and down, and step to the right whilst saying HIE LOST. The dog has seen the dummy fall, knows what your hand signal means and should go and collect the dummy. Now sit the dog. Throw a dummy to nine o'clock. Retreat to six o'clock and signal to the left with your left hand. The dog should collect the dummy. Keep up these retrieves for a few lessons until they are well understood.

Now work on the straight out retrieve. This should not be difficult because it involves the command GET OUT which you have been giving on seen get-back retrieves for a long while now. Sit the dog in the centre of the clock. Throw the dummy to twelve o'clock. Retreat to six o'clock and raise your hand with palm facing forward. Sweep it forward and down, and say GET OUT. The dog should do so and bring the dummy back. All this should not take long because your food-bowl and get-back retrieve training has been going on

Change direction : GO LEFT.

throughout the puppy's infant life, but now you must move to a more difficult phase.

This is take-a-hand-signal-to-an-unseen-dummy. Again you use the clock face technique but before you sit the dog in the clock centre you place a dummy 10 yards at three o'clock and up wind. Retreat to six o'clock hold up your hand and sweep it to the right whilst you step to the right and say HIE LOST. The dog, with the dummy smell strong in its nostrils, should follow your own signal and move off to the retrieve. Repeat with go left and get out retrieves and then stop. Slowness or misunderstandings are dealt with by encouragement and walking the dog to the dummy, but really if the food bowl and other retrieving groundwork have been properly drilled-in these lessons should be taken in their stride. If the early lessons have not been well taught you will waste your time and have much misunderstanding at this stage, and you must, I am afraid, go back to those beginning lessons again.

Retrieve Unseen with Seen in View

Having assured yourself that the dog will go out to any unseen retrieve you must ensure that it will go for an unseen retrieve when

Change direction: GO RIGHT.

Change direction: STOP. *Note the handler's clear signals*

a seen dummy is in view. This is important because on a shooting day at the end of a drive the ground is littered with dead birds lying all round the guns. No dog is needed to pick these birds for they can easily be picked by hand. But before they are picked, runners must be got. These are wounded birds which have run-on, and their recovery is the first priority in the pick-up. A dog must therefore be capable of being sent into the nothingness of an unseen retrieve whilst seen (dead bird) retrieves lie all around. This is a vital piece of gundog work, perhaps one of the most important tasks for which a trained gundog exists. On most shoots dogs will dash around picking the dead birds lying around. This is an exercise in futility and demonstrates the horror of the untrained dog. Alas! most shooting men are unaware of this stupidity and lack of discipline.

To achieve this piece of expertise you need to go back to the food bowl. Prepare the scene beforehand by placing the food bowl on the ground and, away to its left and upwind, place a biscuit. Bring out the dog and sit it equidistant between the bowl and the biscuit and, moving yourself to six o'clock, wave the dog left with a HIE LOST. It will probably hesitate or move towards the food bowl. It must be stopped on the whistle and signalled left vigorously. Each time it moves right to the food bowl it must be stopped, and if necessary you should walk it to the biscuit. A little practice at meal-times and the dog will go left, right or get out to the unseen biscuit with the food bowl in view. You are on your way to unseen with a seen in view. Now you go to the clock face. Place a dummy at nine o'clock, sit the dog in the middle, throw a dummy towards three o'clock, retreat to six o'clock and give the hand signal left with a HIE LOST. The dog should go, but hesitation or movement towards the three o'clock dummy must be dealt with as in the food bowl exercise. Soon unseen dummies in whatever direction should be collected as required.

Double and Multiple Retrieves

On a working day a gundog will be required to collect a multiplicity of game in the order required by the handler. It will probably have seen the birds fall and should have remembered three or four of them. It will also have ideas on the order in which it would like to collect them, and these ideas will almost certainly not accord with those of the handler. So in training there arises the requirement to get used to multiple retrieves of dummies. This is not difficult to teach. Sit the dog and throw a dummy out half-right and another half-left. At first the dog will want to go for the dummy last seen to fall, so send it to the half-left one first. When it brings it back sit it again and then send it for the half-right one. The dog should remember where it fell, but if it hesitates encourage it and if necessary walk it out to the dummy. Soon you will be able to send the dog first to the dummy which fell first and then to the second. This quickly learnt lesson should then be extended to three or four dummies the dog to collect them in any order in which the trainer wishes. *Every dog should have this flexibility of handling before it goes into the field.*

Steady to Diversion

When a dog is hunting to put up game or point if it is a spaniel or pointer, or for a retrieve if it is a retriever, running game may cross its path. *A dog should not chase, but remain steady to, running game.* This is one of the most important lessons that a gundog must learn. The rabbit on the lawn and perhaps visits to the rabbit pen will be used to make the dog steady to ground game, but steadiness to falling or running game must now be learned. As the dog is sent out on a retrieve or on its way back throw another dummy in its path. If it attempts to move towards the thrown dummy shout NO, NO, NO to dissuade it and make absolutely certain that it desists and carries on either to get to or come back with the dummy. Practice should ensure that the dog ignores these diversionary dummies, and from the point of view of future work in the field it is important that it does so. Instead of a thrown dummy, one fired by the dummy launcher to bounce across the dog's path is a very useful variation.

The use of the elasticated rabbit is quite important in training a dog to be steady to diversions. It presents a good simulation of a bolting rabbit, and since it will flash across the dog's front in quite junior working tests it is something worth getting accustomed to as well as being a good training aid. It is simply made by affixing a $1\frac{1}{2}$ lb rabbit-skin-covered dummy by cord to a 10 yard length of $\frac{1}{4}$ in square elastic and securing a peg to another piece of cord attached to the other end of the elastic. The piece of cord should be about 5 yards long, and the peg needs to be capable of remaining firm under strain and holding on in hard and soft earth conditions. Once the dummy is in place and stretched and held by an assistant the dog is sent out on a retrieve and the rabbit released just as the dog passes the line. Any attempt to go to the dummy must be halted, for a tug-of-war with an elasticated rabbit is greatly to be avoided. When this operation is coped with, the rabbit is released ahead of the dog and similar precautions taken against misdemeanour. Then when

German short-haired pointers steady to an elasticated rabbit

all is going well, gunfire at the departing rabbit can be introduced. It is strange how gunfire will hot up a dog, and the handler must be especially vigilant throughout this learning stage.

Introduction to Game

The dummy training which a dog undergoes is preparation for the collection and carrying of game. Gradually a dog must have practice on dummies which approximate to proper game, and fur and feather must be added to the dummies. A rabbit skin dummy should be used after the beginning of retrieving training so that fur in the mouth is something to which it becomes accustomed. To start towards the handling of live birds, feathers, such as pheasant or partridge wings, should be tied to a dummy. The dog may mouth a feather-covered dummy initially, but if the trainer runs away calling-up the dog it will pick up the dummy and come to hand. From now on all dummies should be covered with rabbit skin or feathers. There is a dummy made long and floppy and weighing $2\frac{1}{2}$ lb which is used to give the dog experience of balancing something as long as a hare and carrying it across rough ground and over jumps. This is a useful training aid which I commend.

Now the real thing must be attempted and, out of season when most training takes place, the most probable bird available is wood pigeon. This is not a bird to be used for early practice because its feathers are loose and fill the dog's mouth, something to which dogs take exception and which can put them off for some time. So the pigeon should be put in a stocking to start with. This avoids the loose feathers but gives the dog the feel of game in the mouth. The pigeon should be dead but not stale and should be free of blood. Rabbits, also dead and blood free, should be used too and, just as when feathers were introduced, should the dog mouth its first rabbit, the trainer must run away calling the dog up. These first retrieves of pigeon and rabbit should be short ones and as simple as possible, but retrieves of more complexity should be worked up to and dead game used as much as possible from now on.

Introduction to Shooting

When the shooting season starts the dog should be taken out and kept on the lead. He should be stationed back away from the guns and allowed to absorb the noise and atmosphere of a shooting day and to get used to the fall of birds all around. When the drive is over a simple dead bird should be selected for its first retrieve, and if such a bird is not available then a dead bird should be procured and thrown a short way to make an easy retrieve. The dog may carry its bird awkwardly at first, probably dragging it by the neck. If it does the bird should be placed gently in the dog's mouth, and he should be encouraged to walk around carrying for a while. Very little more should be attempted on this first day, and it should be noted that *a man should not take out his gun on his dog's first day out.* Everything must be concentrated on the dog to make sure all goes off well with no chance of error.

Get Over Obstacles

As the dog grows the 18 in jump which was built for it in its late puppyhood should be raised gradually until it is as high as a five-barred gate, and the dog should be given retrieves regularly over the jump and back. The jump should be steady and the top a firm rung, because although dogs sometimes fly their jumps they more frequently bank them, especially when laden with a heavy bird or a

A puppy learning to jump with a dummy

hare. They often leap to a jump almost vertically and hang on with front paws curled over the top rung, pulling their hind legs up afterwards, so a firm top is necessary. Practice should also be given on jumping high stone walls, for those will be met out shooting and, ferocious though they sometimes look, a good jumping dog will make light of them.

If the dog refuses a jump do not try to force it over, but go back to a jump low enough for it to go over easily; keep practising on that until it regains confidence and then very slowly start to build up the height again. *Every gundog must jump obstacles whether carrying game or not*. There is nothing more degrading than the sight of a gundog being lifted over an obstacle. Such a dog should not be taken out shooting.

The obstacle most frequently encountered by gundogs is barbed wire. If the fence consists only of barbed wire the dog will go through but if the fence is reinforced with chain link fencing or chicken wire the dog must go over. Mostly these fences are jumped clean, but dogs very quickly become adept at banking the top strand and avoiding the barbs, and a trainer should have no hesitation in putting his dog to wire, for it certainly will be faced with it on a shooting day.

Dogs must also be made to get through thick hedges and out on the other side. The dummy should be thrown over the hedge with the dog watching, and from 10 yards away the dog should be sent out with a HIE LOST. As it approaches the hedge it should receive the excited command of GET OVER, OVER, OVER, and this cry should be kept up until the dog forces its way through the bottom of the hedge. Do not take no for an answer, but walk forward until, if necessary, you are standing over the dog and giving the OVER, OVER command. The dog will eventually force its way through, probably crawling on its belly under the thick bottom, and it will certainly find the same, or an easier, way back. Hedges are useful objects for this lesson for they often have overgrown ditches at their bottom; these set another problem for the learner to solve, and they certainly will need to be navigated when the dog is out shooting.

The dog should also be given the opportunity to get out over big stretches of open water and preferably on to an island to retrieve, and then over the island and into open water again. The dummy should be secreted in many hidden directions, for when swimming a dog must swim round to look at its handler when one whistle blast is blown and take a directional hand signal. A dog should be as accurately handleable on water as it is on land, for it will need guiding on to an unseen bird caught under the bank or, in the case of a duck, floating off down stream.

During this training in getting over obstacles the dog must be given retrieves into a wood. Very frequently out shooting birds are put down in a wood surrounded by a thick hedge and heavily undergrown with bramble. This is a situation in which a gundog really is required to do its stuff, and it needs practice in it if it is not to run up and down the edge of the wood in a distracted way when asked to go and get a bird. It is this sort of situation which separates out the good dogs from the bad. The average dog out shooting refuses to get in, and this results in a lost bird and the owner having to force his way through the tangle to lead the dog to the retrieve. Both outcomes are most undesirable and very frequently to be seen. To make sure that your dog is not such a one it must have the opportunity to practice this sort of retrieve. Find a good brambly piece of covert with a difficult entry. Sit the dog 10 yards from the edge and let it see you lob the dummy into the wood. Go back to the dog and send it off to retrieve. It should force its way in and hunt for the dummy. You will not be able to give it any guidance, and so it will have to hunt on its own initiative. This it will have to do very frequently when out shooting, for retrieving on a shooting day is very rarely a matter of whistle and hand signal but more a matter of get in and hunt. This must be practised in artificial conditions so that it will be performed on a working day. From now on such retrieves should be carried out unseen so that the dog's initiative will be tested to the full.

Training Classes

I strongly recommend that during its formal training period a dog should be taken to training classes with its local gundog society. The name of your nearest and most appropriate society can be obtained from the Kennel Club, and such societies normally run training classes throughout the non-shooting season. They also run competitive working tests out of season and field trials during the season. All these activities I recommend in the building up of a good gundog.

The training classes, usually on a Sunday afternoon, are very valuable to the lone trainer, for they provide an otherwise unobtainable opportunity for your dog to mix with other dogs, something it will have to do out shooting. At first your dog will almost certainly pull on its lead to try to sniff at and play with the other dogs, and this is a wonderful opportunity for it to be pulled back to heel when walking or to sit when you are standing still in a bunch. There will be a class for beginners and classes for more advanced dogs all under command of an experienced trainer, and you can try your dog out on new territory and in the presence of many people and dogs. This is an essential type of learning, and it is absolutely vital that the dog gets used to this bustle before it is taken out shooting. If it goes straight from the loneliness of the training ground to the commotion of a shooting day disaster will almost certainly ensue. This is, too, an opportunity to compare your dog's performance – and your own – with others engaged in the same training exercise, to exchange views with them and to get advice from the class commander: all most valuable. You can work your way up through the various working tests, and even if you do not win you and your dog will gain experience approximating to shooting conditions with gunfire, people, dogs, water work, unseen retrieves and diversions, experience only got through a gundog society.

Problems

There are some problems revealed in training that are fatal to success and some which can be overcome. Fatal to the production of a gundog and rightly the cause of instant dismissal from a field trial are running-in, whimpering or otherwise giving tongue and hard-mouth.

Hard-mouth is probably hereditary. A hard-mouthed dog brings back a bird with the rib cage crushed. If you hold the bird with its breast bone resting in the palm of your hand you can feel its collapsed, almost jellified, state. A bird may of course have crashed into a tree or the ground or have needed fierce pulling from tough cover by the dog and thus have been damaged; so judges, who must agree together that the fault of hard-mouth exists, usually give the dog the benefit of the first doubt and eliminate it only when the fault is confirmed. There are ways of attempting to cure hard-mouth. It may be apparent on the dummy that the dog is ramming its teeth in or hanging on with a vice-like grip at hand-over, and squeezing the dog's lips on to its teeth to make it release the dummy is one method which might change its habits. It is sometimes suggested that a dummy covered with hedgehog skin or with sharp spikes sticking out may convince the dog that tender carrying of the dummy is to be preferred. I think that a well-bred gundog has a mouth as soft as velvet and balances its game with the delicacy of a wine waiter carrying a tray of glasses. Hard-mouth is an aberration and an irreversible fact in my view, and the dog that has it is a waste of time.

A gundog should never give tongue and most of them never do. The fault, if it exists, usually first shows itself when the dog is in the line. At this time with guns going off and game falling all around dogs can get very excited. The phlegmatic take it in their stride, but the highly strung can start whimpering and even, when they get really steamed-up, can start barking. Out shooting it is not unusual to find a gun out with a dog barking. Unfortunately shooting men little understand dog work and seem impervious to the appalling behaviour of their dog. In the old days the host would have ordered the dog away, and perhaps even its accompanying gun too, for such misbehaviour; but alas! shooting mores are changing, and today to hear a dog barking throughout the day is not unusual. If your dog evinces this unfortunate whining habit you must chop it across the jaw with the side of your hand, grip its jaws tight shut and say NO, NO, NO. Every tiniest sound of a whimper must be the cause of a stern chop and verbal disapproval. Many dogs overcome this fault when they are treated thus, although the handler may remain tense with apprehension for a long time after its apparent cure in case an exciting stand may bring it back. If the fault is incurable the dog is useless for training purposes.

There is little that the reader of these pages needs to be told about running in. I have said that it is an unforgivable fault, and all my training is aimed at ensuring that it does not develop. If when put to the test your dog runs-in, whether in competition or out shooting, you must go back to the beginning and start steadying the dog all over again. This often has to be done, but if retraining proves unsuccessful, then give up the training of that dog and get another.

During training there are frequently problems over retrieving. The most usual ones are that the dog refuses to go out when sent, that it refuses to pick up the dummy, that it drops the dummy on the way back and that it circles around the trainer refusing to hand over the dummy. These are usually signs that the trainer has bored the dog with over-retrieving. When the dog circles round the trainer it is a sign that it does not find it pleasurable to hand over the dummy probably because it has been snatched from its mouth or taken over hastily by the trainer. The problem can usually be solved by squatting down whilst the dog circles round, patting the floor and encouraging the dog to come. When it does the dummy should be taken gently and handed back to the dog's mouth at once and the dog called to heel and allowed to carry the dummy for quite a while. From then on you should carry out this drill until the dog comes right up to hand, when it should be sat at the hand-over and then have the dummy placed back in its mouth and left there for a while. When the dog gets used to receiving the dummy back after each retrieve it should overcome its reluctance to hand over.

When the dog drops the dummy on the return the trainer should run away blowing the three recall whistle blasts and continue even if it means disappearing from sight. The dog should pick up the dummy and follow.

When a dog refuses to pick the dummy or refuses to go out for it, all retrieving training must be stopped. The dog should be given the dummy to play with and carry around from time to time but not over frequently, and it should be waved temptingly under its nose whilst encouraging noises are made. After several weeks of this abstinence from retrieving a small seen retrieve of great simplicity may be tried. If it is carried out successfully do not be tempted to try another and another. Stop and wait until the next day before you try again.

Punishment

By and large the training of a gundog does not involve the administration of punishment. When a puppy gets things wrong it is almost always because it does not understand. It does not understand either because it is too unintelligent and therefore no amount of chastisement will make it understand, or because the trainer has failed to give it the message he is trying to communicate, in which case it is logically the trainer who should be punished, not the dog.

It is necessary, however, to indicate to a dog that it is doing wrong and must desist. This is mostly conveyed by tone of voice, for a dog reacts absolutely to the voice that it hears. If you talk soothingly to your dog it will wag its tail with delight, as it recognises that its pack leader is pleased. Conversely if you speak harshly to the dog it will lower its tail and show sorrow and fear. Mostly, therefore, when your dog misbehaves a very gruffly spoken NO should make it think very hard before it carries on with the same behaviour. You can if you like express displeasure with a stream of gruff expletives, and although the dog will not understand a syllable it will get the message that you do not like what it is, or was, up to.

Punishment in retrospect is quite useless with a dog and can only cause bewilderment. *A dog should be corrected only at the time and at the place of misbehaviour.* If you leave your dog indoors and come home to find some precious possession destroyed it is useless to vent your spleen on the dog. It will long have forgotten that it did wrong and will connect your appearance with the punishment to the great detriment of your future meetings. If on the other hand you enter the room and find the destruction taking place a rating there and then will be connected in the dog's mind with the misbehaviour. If your dog runs off you must never chide it on its return. It will connect the punishment with the return, not with its running off. But if you can see your dog's muscles bunched for a run-in or a chase and you can get to it at that moment it will understand your rating, for it will be connected with the evil thought it has in its mind. Whatever your dog brings to you must be taken tenderly and with much praise. It must not be snatched because it is too precious to be in the dog's mouth, and the dog must never get the feeling that you expressed displeasure at its bringing you something. Everything must be brought to you always and accepted with a show of pleasure.

As to punishment, it can be administered, but in special ways. In the nineteenth century dogs were thrashed with whips in training, and far from having a prolonged period of dummy work they were taken straight into the field and thrashed for doing wrong. Richard Sharpe, the father of modern training methods, wrote: 'Nowadays a trainer should carry nothing in his hands so that the temptation to hit a dog does not arise. Dogs in training are usually hit in anger and this is fatal to the success of the enterprise.' *Good trainers do not lose their temper.* Displeasure needs, with a very stubborn dog, to be shown with some vigour on occasions. All our training is Pavlovian because we are dealing with conditioned reflexes, and it is important that some undesirable actions are connected with an unpleasant result. Again it must be emphasised that punishment should take place only on the spot and at the time of the misdemeanour. The method of punishment is based on that shown by a dog's mother or its pack-leader. Habitually bitches stop puppies from misbehaving by picking them up in their mouth by the scruff of the neck, and pack-leaders defend their leadership in fighting by attacking the throat, the lip and the ear. We do all these things to impress upon a dog that it is doing wrong. If it moves forward from the spot on which it has been told to wait we pick it up by the slack flesh around its throat and carry it back. If it runs-in we bring it back to the spot from which it set-off, scruff it by the neck and tweak its ear and its lip. These things should be done with discrimination and only when the dog will certainly know for what it is being chastised. But by and large successful training is carried out by repetition and association of action with pleasure, and of course the shortest way to a dog's heart is down its throat with a titbit for its stomach.

CHAPTER SEVEN

Special Training for Spaniels

A spaniel needs the same initial cossetting as a retriever for its first 6 months and should emerge with the same disciplines. Its training must now diverge from that of the retriever for it must learn to quarter its ground as well as to retrieve. Different dogs are ready for this part of their training at different ages, and no hard and fast rule can be laid down as to the desirability of pushing ahead. The trainer must assess whether it is too soon to start work on a dog at 6 months or whether it can be set on its programmed training at 5 months. My word of advice is that it is better to be too late than too soon, for starting too soon can be ruinous. A spaniel must drop to the flush of game, to gunshot and to the fall of game. Until this steadiness is imparted no further progress can be made. This is again the lynchpin of the training programme and *a spaniel must drop to flush, gun and fall before it can make progress.*

Steadiness

How to get to this steadiness is a nice problem with a spaniel because above all it must hunt. That is its purpose in life, and the end product will be a dog that quarters its ground with energy and bustle and in the process thrashes through covert however obdurate that may be. So having a very steady spaniel which sticks to its owner's side is no achievement at all, even though with a retriever such a result might not be undesirable.

Spaniel puppies should be encouraged to hunt from an early age by being allowed to run around places full of game smells. Some trainers go further than this and positively encourage dogs to chase, their theory being that it is better to know that the dog will hunt and have to slow it down than the opposite, which is to try to encourage a sticky unresponsive dog to hunt – a nice dilemma. I think I go along with the great H. W. Carlton, whose book *Spaniels: their breaking for sport or field trials* was first published in 1914 and is now in its ninth edition. He wrote contemptuously of the advocates of 'letting your puppy run wild and chase if opportunity offers, up to the age of as much as twelve months'. 'Dropping,' he said, 'is, in fact, of

A little spaniel shows its strength with a large hare

the very essence of good spaniel breaking.' Keith Erlandson, a modern spaniel expert, is not averse to encouraging free hunting in a puppy and steadying it down later, but nevertheless he writes: 'If I were to be asked which, in my opinion, is the most important lesson of all, I would reply, without hesitation, that to teach a dog to sit and stay is the most vital lesson of all.' So I think that it would be as well if the majority of spaniels in training were taught this lesson in steadiness before being sent out hunting live game.

A spaniel's specialised job is to push up game – not to point it or dash into cover and peg it (that is to say, pick it up), but to push it up with its nose, diving forward into the seat of the game, whether wing or fur, until it flies or runs. As the game takes off the spaniel must sit or at least stop absolutely. This seeking of game must be carried out in a methodical manner, leaving no likely cover un-investigated and putting up no game out of gunshot. It is these two requirements which dictate the method a spaniel must use in its hunting and therefore the manner of training it.

Pattern

The extreme limit of a shotgun's range is about 40 yards; its certain killing range is a little more than 30 yards. Game must be flushed within that range if it is to be shootable, and therefore it is useless for a dog to hunt further out than about 25 yards in any direction from its following gun. The dog must hunt back and forth in front of its gun 25 yards to the left, turn, cross in front, and go 25 yards to the right before turning again. The scent given off by a bird, rabbit or hare travels quite a short distance, and on a bad scenting day an extremely short distance, so when the dog reaches its 25 yard turning point it must not move too far forward before coming across again, otherwise it will leave a strip of uninvestigated ground between its lines of hunting. An advance of 10–15 yards at each turn is about right.

This manner of ground treatment is known as the pattern, and whilst many spaniels are almost instinctive in patterned hunting it is a lesson which needs teaching to most dogs. The method is simple but it can be a lesson long in learning to perfection. Unless a dog is firm in its drop to a whistle blast and free from chase, the lesson is almost unteachable, as once it starts hunting a dog is often tempted to follow a rabbit's foot trail from its seat to its burrow or a pheasant's or partridge's long run forward, for both birds are reluctant to fly. These are things a good spaniel must never do, for they result in a flush out of range, if not the flush of much game passed *en route.*

On its 25 yard patrol the dog must investigate those foot scents, note their existence and stick to its hunting pattern until the game is hunted to its seat for flushing within gunshot.

Quartering

The introduction to quartering is made by the handler facing the wind – and all early hunting should be into the wind so that game smells are brought to the dog's nose – and walking the dog 25 yards left. At that extremity the dog's attention should be attracted by two peeps on the whistle or a SSST, and with a wave of the arm as the trainer turns right the dog should be cast right. At 25 yards to the

Two springers hunting out a rough corner

right of a central point – or 50 yards from the left extremity – the whistle peep-peep, SSST or click of the fingers – whatever sign you intend to use to turn your dog when out working – should be given and the left arm swung left. Gradually the dog should understand what is required of it, and you should in due course be able, instead of walking back and forth encouraging the dog, to walk forward in a straight line sending and turning the dog right and left and the 25 yard limit. If the dog seems unable to react to this controlled quartering it should be put on a check-cord, pulled round at the turning point and led across in the required direction. It is much to be hoped that this will not be necessary, for the check-cord's use precludes operating in well-covered ground and entails the return to flat meadowland where the check-cord will not get snarled up in every obstacle.

This pursuit of a good pattern is not to be confused with the spaniels' job of bashing into cover. Just to motor along in straight lines making a perfect pattern is useless. Along its line of hunting the dog must investigate every bit of cover in case some game is *in situ*. This must produce a ragged back-and-forth hunting pattern and it is the quintessence of spaniel work: bustle, bustle from bracken to thorn to tussock to whin, in and through and out, driving into tough brambles, shrugging aside every obstacle. That is the perfect spaniel action with stem working vigorously all the while and getting up to unbelievable speed when on to a scent – a great thrill for the working handler especially if he is armed with a shotgun.

But one must come back to that 25 yard pattern, and although every piece of cover must be investigated the dog must turn at 25 yards however thrilling the scent may be at that moment. Useless to carry on an excited hunt for 45 yards to flush game out of gunshot. The game to be flushed is all that is lying up within the handler's range, and to work on that restricted front is what a spaniel must be taught to do.

Enter Cover

It will need to be taught to get into cover from an early age, for no puppy instinctively relishes plunging into thick brambles, but either by steady progress from prickleless bracken or by following the example of an old dog a spaniel must learn to enjoy entering cover. Initial fear may be overcome by letting the dog see you throw in a biscuit, when its stomach will almost certainly take it in to retrieve. Gradually the tempting morsel is thrown into thicker and thicker cover. This habit of investigating cover must become a reflex with a spaniel and must be added on to the training to turn at 25 yards and to cross in front of the gun on a path not many yards further on.

Gone Away

During this hunting the dog will at some stage – perhaps, to your consternation, very early in the course – put up game. As the game departs the dog should sit. You will shoot at the game. If you kill it the dog should mark and stay seated. In early training days you would be wise to go and pick that shot game yourself, but in due course the dog sitting to the shot will be sent to retrieve game that we hope it has marked down. All this should be carried out without error, and so it will be if your steadiness lessons are well implanted. You may fire and miss the game, and this is something that will happen frequently in the field. At this moment the dog is sitting tense in anticipation of a retrieve. All that is in fact required of him is that he should put his nose down and go on hunting. You must at this moment give the important command GONE AWAY. This should mean to the dog: 'Forget that incident and continue hunting.' It is a very important lesson: it can fairly easily be taught to a steady dog and is murder to teach to a dog with a propensity to run-in to shot.

Make absolutely sure that the firing of a shot is a signal to your dog to sit. This of course is basic hand breaking but is often skipped over with fatal results. Every time a dummy launcher or a gun is fired a dog must be taught to sit so that to do so is a reflex. You can imagine how vital it is that a spaniel stops in its tracks when a shot is fired, and at that moment the command GONE AWAY is of great importance.

Spaniels have an endearing habit when working in high cover of standing up on their hind legs when a shot is fired in an attempt to see ahead and mark the fall. As long as this action is followed by the dog sitting or standing stock still and looking back at its handler for the next instruction it is much to be encouraged, for it shows a desire to mark, and marked game is much more easily collected than unmarked, on to the fall of which the dog needs directing.

Wind Direction

All early hunting lessons must be carried out into the wind, and the earliest pattern with the handler walking right and left with the dog will be something like Figure 1, where the dotted line shows the

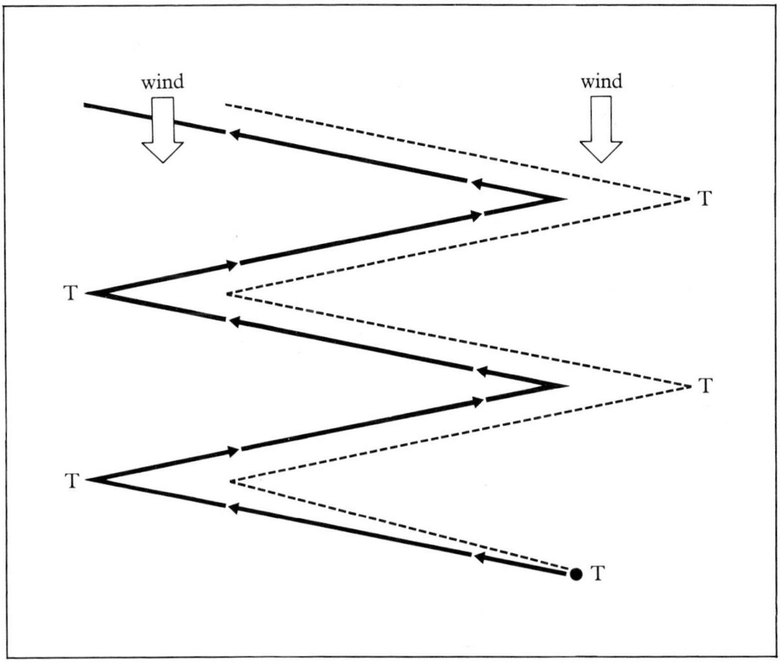

Figure 1

handler's path and T the point at which the dog's direction is changed.

The proper pattern to which a dog should work into the wind allows the gun to walk steadily forward in a straight line with the dog questing 25 yards right and left so that all game discovered in the beat is shootable. That pattern is shown in Figure 2. Remember that those straight lines will not be adhered to, for the dog's job is to investigate all cover along the way so that his progress will be a series of quick dashes from tussock to bramble looking for game as in Figure 3.

When the dog is good at hunting into the wind – and not until this is well done always – it should be introduced to hunting down wind or into side quartering winds. These call for differing quartering patterns so that the dog hunts into the wind although it is not blowing towards the gun. With a following wind the technique is for the dog to go out ahead of the gun and work back into the wind towards the advancing gun (Figure 4).

The dog must hunt back close to the handler before being cast forward to turn again into the wind otherwise much ground will be

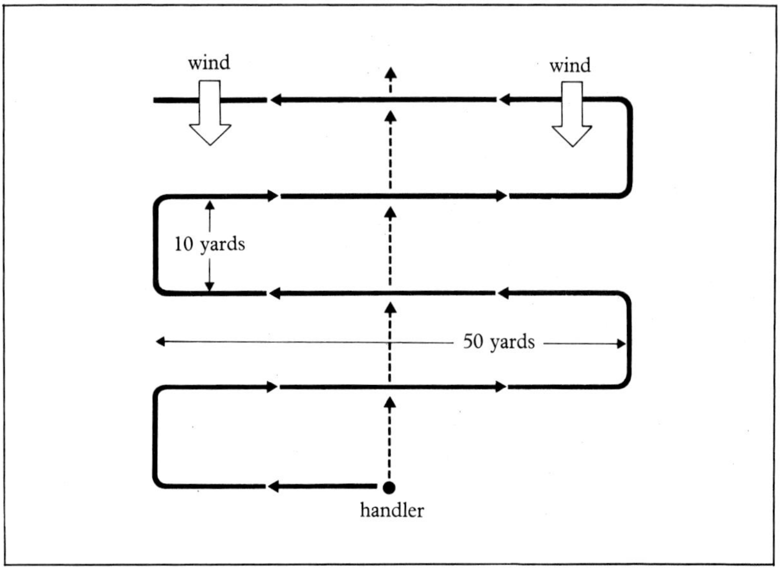

Figure 2

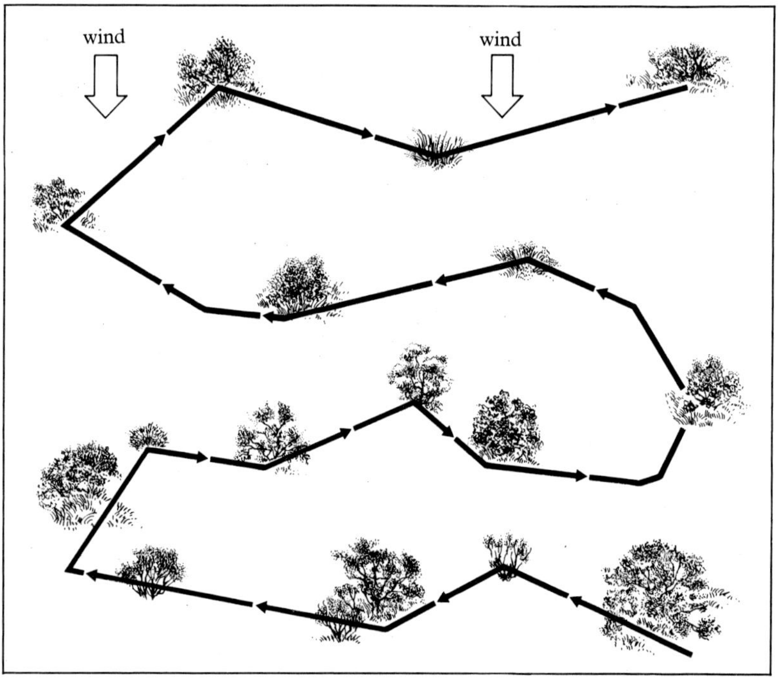

Figure 3

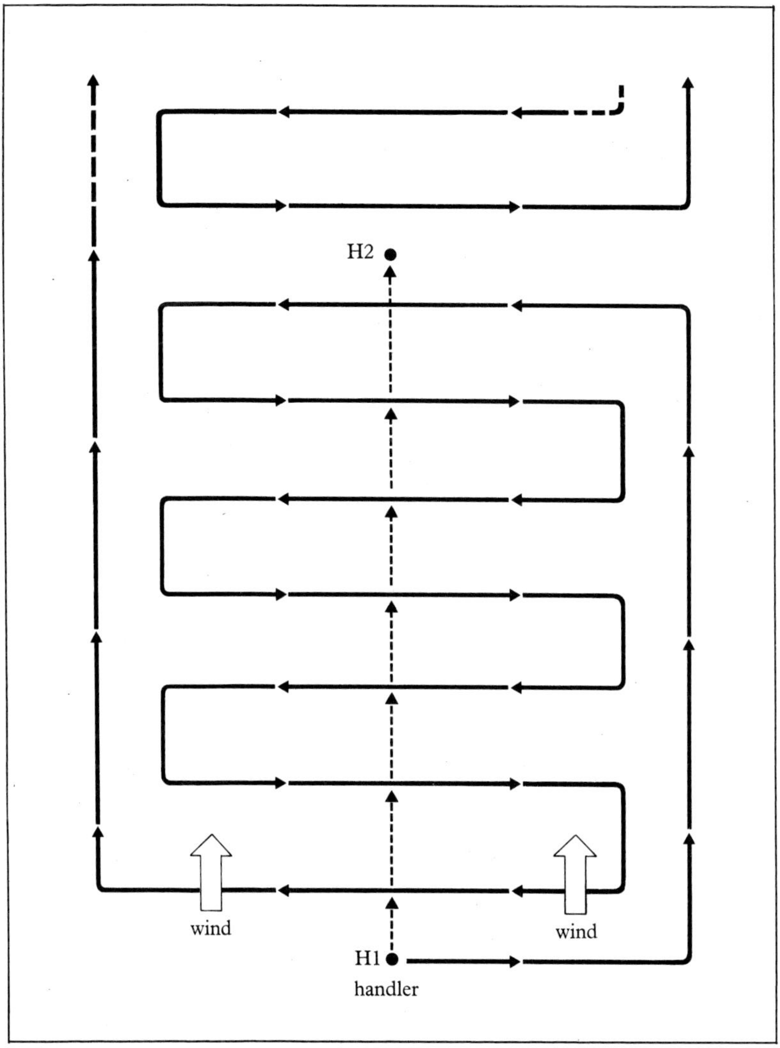

Figure 4

missed. The handler walks forward to a point (H2) the distance of the dog's cast forwards.

Hunting with a cross wind involves a tricky staccato technique which calls for much turning of the dog set to hunt in an unaccustomed way. The pattern, which needs a good deal of practice should look like Figure 5. This keeps the dog head into wind and leaves no missed ground – a pretty manoeuvre to watch.

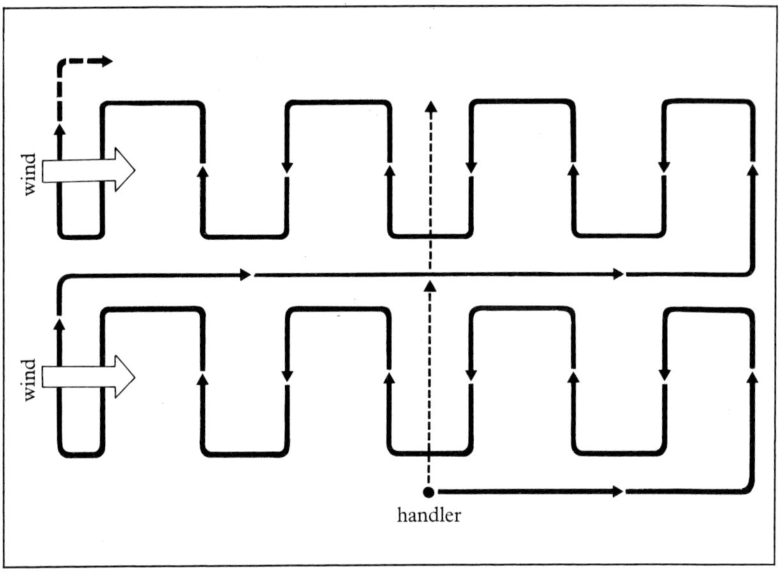

Figure 5

Retrieving, water work and jumping are taught to spaniels as they are taught to retrievers, but the addition of hunting and sitting to flush, shot and game makes spaniel training an especially interesting task.

CHAPTER EIGHT

Special Training for Pointers and Setters

Pointers and setters do not retrieve. They seek out game and indicate its presence by standing still staring at the birds, holding them in position by eye from a distance. That distance will depend upon scenting conditions, for on a good scenting day the dog hunting with its head held high in the air feeling the wind for game-smells may come on point (as the standing still is called) 50 yards or more from the game.

A wide grouse moor is the place for a setter and a pointer, though they both – and especially a pointer – may be used on the more restricted ground of stubbles in pursuit of partridges. It is in fact no bad thing to start a dog off on partridges and then move on to grouse, for grouse have a strong scent and, getting used to that, the dog may find partridge scent uninteresting.

Method of Hunting

One dog in the field should work for three guns, not more, and those guns should walk behind the handler, and therefore behind the working dog too, until the dog comes on point when they should gather around the dog with guns ready for the flushed bird. The dog, given the freedom of the moor, should hunt across on a front 300 yards wide. This is the distance which would be covered by six or seven walking guns spaced out in line and, since a dogging moor, as it is called, contains not enough game to accommodate so many guns the dog's patrol will enable three guns to have the opportunity of shooting all the birds on a seven-man front. The dog should cover its ground quickly, as it does normally with its long racing stride, and should turn through 180 degrees at the end of its beat, move forward about 15 yards and work back across the front of the handler and guns as they advance on a line across the middle of, and at right angles to, the dog's beat.

Drop to Signal

Pointers and setters have an instinct to point or sett (which derives from 'sit' in the days when setters lay down as they located game so

Good discipline: a pointer stays down while its companion is cast out

that nets could be thrown over dog and covey). They should also have an instinct to carry their head high when hunting, feeling the wind for scent. Therefore, in a good dog bred from shooting, and not show, blood lines these instincts should need very little working on in training to bring them out as working tools.

Like all dogs, however, pointers and setters have an instinct to chase. A dog which chases is quite worthless in the field, and so it is, as always in dog training, absolutely vital that, before live game is hunted, the dog is trained to be rock steady to the movement of fur, wing, sheep or deer. A very famous book on 'Breaking or Training the English Spaniel or Pointer', called *Kunopaedia*, written in 1814 by William Dobson, made the point for all trainers to remember forever. 'Down Charge' was the command used in those days to make a dog drop, and this is what Dobson wrote about teaching 'Down Charge': 'Sir, it is that of the highest importance in the whole of my system of education; the great hinge upon which all its future refinements rest.' It is the same today: a pointer or setter must, before it is allowed to hunt, be taught to drop to the flush of birds, the shooting of a gun, the verbal command – whatever is chosen, one whistle blast and the raised hand – and it must react to all those things by thumping down to a halt and waiting until told to do otherwise.

So we see again that the initial training of a pointing dog, destined though it may be to gallop freely over the moor, is, like that of its completely opposite companion the non-slip retriever or its near cousin the flushing spaniel, to be completely steady and the same lessons in WAIT, STAY, COME, HEEL, GO LEFT, GO RIGHT and GET ON must be given with the food bowl as a useful adjunct (see pages 99–100). A pointer must walk calmly on the lead, not pulling its handler's arm out of its socket, but it is unwise to teach heeling until the dog's instinct to hunt has been developed, otherwise a dog may become too sticky – that is, reluctant to move forward from its handler's side.

When this early steadiness training (and it includes GET IN THE CAR/KENNEL and BED and BUSY) is well inculcated the dog may start its more advanced training to teach it to quarter its ground in a regular and controlled manner. The ultimate object of the lesson is to teach the dog to move across country on a 300 yard front taking forward 'bites' of ground into the wind (depending on scenting conditions) of from 10 to 25 yards at the end of its range and back across the front of the handler. If on its galloping patrol it scents game it should come to point. When the handler and guns arrive and are in position, it should move forward towards the game (this forward movement is known as 'roading') and flush the birds for the guns to shoot. At flush and shot the dog should go down. If the pointed game is suspected to be a covey the dog moves around after the first shot 'making out the covey' and so points birds which are still sitting tight. That is almost the completion of the dog's work, following which it is cast off again to continue quartering.

To Ho

A pointer may not rush forward and flush birds before the arrival of the guns. It is their instinct so to do, and the first lesson after steadiness – and this should probably not be before the dog is 6 months old – is the lesson of TO HO. It is hardly necessary to explain that a dog has no vocabulary or powers of reasoning, so the commands to which it responds may be any which the trainer cares to select. A dog will sit to the command STAND if it is taught so to do. Orders to a gundog should be given in staccato and unvarying language, and one of the nonsense words used for pointers is TO HO. It is the word used to stop a dog as it scents birds and before it flushes them. It is a steadiness lesson and must be absolutely firmly instilled, for a pointer which will run into its birds is a disaster and useless.

This lesson is carried out on a check-cord and is important but simple. A cord 7 or 8 yards long is looped round the dog's neck. The handler is prepared with a pocketful of biscuit, liver, cheese, anything the dog will gladly eat. A new command is introduced as the dog is shown the titbit: DEAD. Henceforth that will mean, 'Here comes something worth investigating', such as a covey seen by the handler. Now it means, 'Here's this nice edible thing.' When the dog has seen it, the bait is thrown, and the puppy rushes after it. For five or six times it is allowed to go straight to the bait and eat it,

A Weimaraner pointing a grouse

the check cord just slipping through the trainer's hand (he should always wear a strong leather glove whenever the dog is on a check-cord). Next the bait is thrown, the dog follows and, some feet before it reaches the food, the handler stops it on the check-cord and says TO HO. When the puppy is calm, having recovered from its surprise and its attempts to struggle forward, the command ON is given, the check-cord is released and the dog rushes to the bait. Be sure the dog goes out with zest and stops only at the TO HO, not in anticipation. Dogs vary in their speed of learning the TO HO lesson, but to stop in full flight must become a reflex before you can go further with training.

At the same time directional hand signals can be taught without the dog realising it by the handler's tossing the biscuits with an arm wave in differing directions.

Quartering

Now your dog is steady at the drop to whistle, hand signal, voice and shot. He can be dropped when moving away or towards you and when ranging right and left, and he will TO HO when called upon to do so. Quartering must now be taught, first on flat game-less ground and into the wind. The signal for turning when out quartering is two whistle blasts and a hand signal given by waving the arm in the direction to be followed. Initially quite short quartering patterns of, say 30 or 40 yards should be used, and the handler should cast the dog off with a hand wave and follow the direction on foot himself. At 20 yards to the left the handler should give two peeps on the whistle to attract the dog's attention and wave him right whilst setting off walking right himself. The dog should follow. If he does, go 40 yards right and repeat the procedure. If the dog responds, and such is the instinct of a well-bred pointer so to do that it may well, then a great deal of anguish is over, for a gradual extension of the range can be embarked upon, and soon the dog will automatically turn to two peeps on the whistle. You are in business with a biddable dog and may expect to teach the rest of the dog's curriculum without difficulty.

But all is not always well. When set off to range some dogs rush off in an uncontrolled gallop and are over the hill and far away in a flash. Never chase such a dog. Rather hide yourself, relying on its distress at being lost to bring it back, and then have recourse to the long check-cord. This is an efficacious if boring procedure. Attach a 50 yard cord to the dog's collar, send it out to the left; when it has gone 25 or 50 yards give two peeps on the whistle and pull the dog through 180 degrees, waving your arm right. The dog should respond to the check-cord's pressure and start to go right. At 25 yards right, peep-peep, pull round, wave and hope that the dog responds and comes hunting across your front. It should, and in time it will.

A good dog will move across the wind 'feeling' it with its nostrils as it glides across. Some dogs 'bore' forward (a technical term meaning to hunt in a straight line forward into the wind) instead of hunting across. Here the check-cord is a help because the dog can be pulled across by pressure every time it moves straight forward. Practice should soon make perfect, and you can first shorten the check-cord, letting the dog drag it freely, and then dispense with it. Any transgression and it is back to the check-cord, I am afraid, but if this is too prolonged you probably have a dog not worthwhile persisting with.

Teaching a dog a good quartering pattern is of the utmost importance, and it can take several months to get to the stage where a dog's pattern is near perfect whatever the topography of the land. Where, for instance, there are root crops drilled in rows it is a temptation to the dog to run straight down a row boring into the wind, missing game on either side and getting out of range; or natural features like drains, ditches and hedges may draw the dog's attention from its perfect pattern. On a grouse moor there is less danger of these false hunting distractions, but nevertheless keeping a good pattern should be watched for on the moor as well as on stubble and in roots, for this is not instinctive in the dog and has to be imprinted by hard and long training. Not that one training session should be long; 'short and often' is as always to be recommended, but the frustrations of this lesson can be many. Ideally when it gets to the end of its cast the dog should, at two whistle peeps, turn through 90 degrees and set off in the opposite direction to its previous course. At first a dog may be inclined to turn through 180 degrees and move off diagonally across the handler's front not making good his 25 yard advance until the end of the beat and thus leaving much ground unworked (Figure 6).

To avoid this the handler should turn from his forward-facing advance to face the dog as it nears the end of its beat and on two peeps of the whistle give, as the dog looks up, a definite hand signal to go right (or left) – that is, forward along the line of your advance – then, 25 yards on, peep-peep and facing forward again wave the dog across right or left. Constant repetition of this stop, go, stop, go lesson should get the dog on a constant hunting pattern consisting of two right angled turns and not one 180 degree turn.

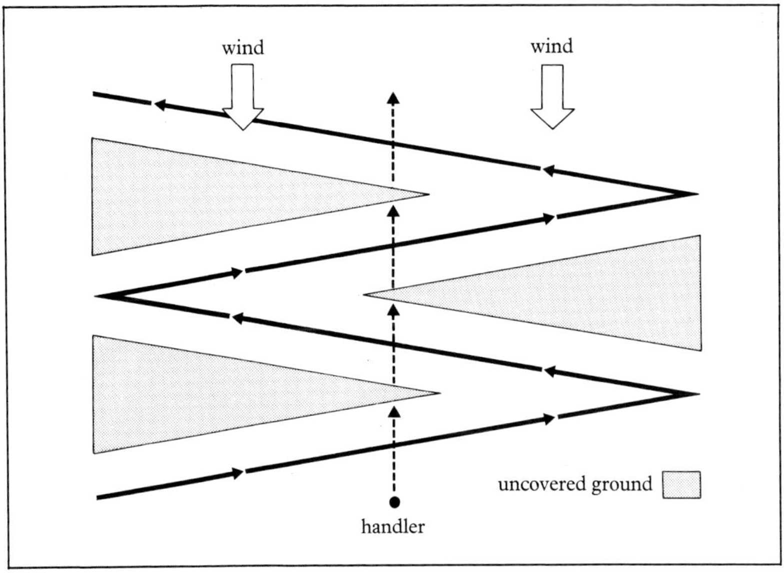

Figure 6

Another movement which may need teaching is the turn forward into the wind at the end of the beat. Many dogs go forward at one end and backwards towards or behind the handler at the other. This is a useless manoeuvre and must be stamped out by whistling and signalling; it may be helped by the handler moving 25 yards forward of the dog's line so that he has to pull forward to catch up. This of course is not a method for use in the field because the handler may walk into birds on unhunted ground.

Pointing

It can be of great benefit to give the dog experience of live birds in a controlled manner before taking it into the field, and for this purpose keeping a loft of half a dozen homing pigeons has much to commend it. A pigeon with its head tucked under its wing will, when turned round and round with a circular movement, become dizzy (indeed the procedure is called 'dizzying') and will then be quiescent for a considerable time when placed on the ground.

The dog can be brought to such a bird and the whole lesson of point, TO HO, ON and DOWN can be practised. The pigeon when flushed will return to its roost, and a good and educational time may be had by all. The only snag in this otherwise splendid arrangement is that the pigeons are often so uncooperative as to recover their

A Hungarian Viszla coming to point on a pigeon in a trap

senses and fly off before the dog gets to them. To overçome this the pigeons are sometimes placed in wire traps which can be sprung by pulling a string, so that when their hidden presence is pointed by the dog he can be moved forward, the string pulled and the bird flushed. The slight disadvantage is that the dog may point and become steady to the trap, not the bird, and still need educating on live birds when he is moved into the field.

The time has now come for work on wild birds. Before contemplating such a big and hazardous move, *the dog must be absolutely steady to fur, wing, shot and, above all, TO HO, and its quartering must be so sound that there can be no question of getting out of control.* What now has to be confirmed, in the presence of game, is that as the dog starts to 'feather' (a technical word indicating the moment when, coming on scent, the dog slows up, crouches, moves in short bursts and waves its tail furiously) he will respond to TO HO and stop. A dog well disciplined in hand training should do so, but if it rushes forward and flushes the bird in spite of your TO HO entreaties you must get to the dog quickly, scold it with a flow of loud TO HO's, drag it by its neck-flesh back to the spot it should have stopped at and keep it there for several minutes. If such appalling behaviour is persisted in, you may have to use the long check-cord to hold the dog on point and then restrain it as you give the command ON to the flush. It is, however, a great setback to have to use a check-cord on live game, and progress will be slow henceforth.

A dog being stroked to drop as a bird is flushed

A dog sits to a shot

Drop to Shot

When pointing, and holding to the point until the handler arrives and gives the ON, is perfect, a head of game should be shot. You are coming up to the last big lesson – steadiness to shot. As you shoot the bird watch the dog and see that it drops, or give the command

SIT, WAIT, HUP, or DOWN or blow one whistle blast. If the dog stops and watches the falling bird, practice should make perfect; but if the dog runs-in to the killed bird you must once again get to it, drag it back to the position from which it ran, rate it, blow the whistle, shout HUP or whatever and keep it there for a long time. It may be that you will again have to have recourse to the check-cord, and this may eventually work; but for your sake I hope it is unnecessary as it should be if your basic training was sound.

Dead Bird

The last lesson of all is not a big one and should produce no trouble. If you are without a retriever you need to find shot game, and so the pointer is trained to 'road' onwards and point the dead bird. It should not be difficult to signal towards the bird in the required direction (walking that way yourself initially) and TO HO the dog as it points. A dog may go forward and mouth the game and must be dissuaded from so doing, but soon it should carry out this last task well. Having done it the dog watches the handler pick the bird, which he should do with a display of much pleasure, and responds to the next hand signal to cast off on a new patrol.

Blinking

A pointer/setter fault which may occur and which is almost always trainer-induced is 'blinking': that is, refusing to point and in fact sometimes returning to the handler's side when game is scented. The cause of this is too severe rating of the dog when it moves forward before TO HO or before ON, so that the thought of being on point fills the dog with alarm: it expects to be punished for moving forward and so refuses to put itself in the initial position, the point, from which, in its mind, the trouble stems. This fault can only be overcome by much kindness, stroking, cossetting and soft speech when the dog is on the point. It must be taught to lose its fear of TO HO and ON.

Another possible reason for blinking is gun-shyness, and this can be overcome only by having shots fired at a distance and making much of the dog whilst giving it a titbit. Gradually (but over many days) the shooting can be brought closer until with luck the dog should calm down to gunshot and stay on point instead of cringing away.

Wind direction

Ideally a dog should always hunt into the wind, for it is the wind which brings scent to a dog's nostrils. Unfortunately it is not always possible for the handler and guns to walk straight into the wind; but still the ground needs hunting, and this gives rise to the necessity to train the dog to use differing quartering patterns in differing wind situations.

The variations from a direct hunt into the wind are when the wind blows from behind the guns or from the side across the face of the guns. In down-wind quartering (Figure 4, p. 149) the handler moves up across the hunted country to H2 before sending the dog out on a further 60 yard sweep. In cheek-wind quartering (Figure 7) a diagonal pattern is used.

Backing

The last lesson of all for setters and pointers is to learn to 'back' a pointing dog when they work in pairs. It is a steadiness lesson fairly

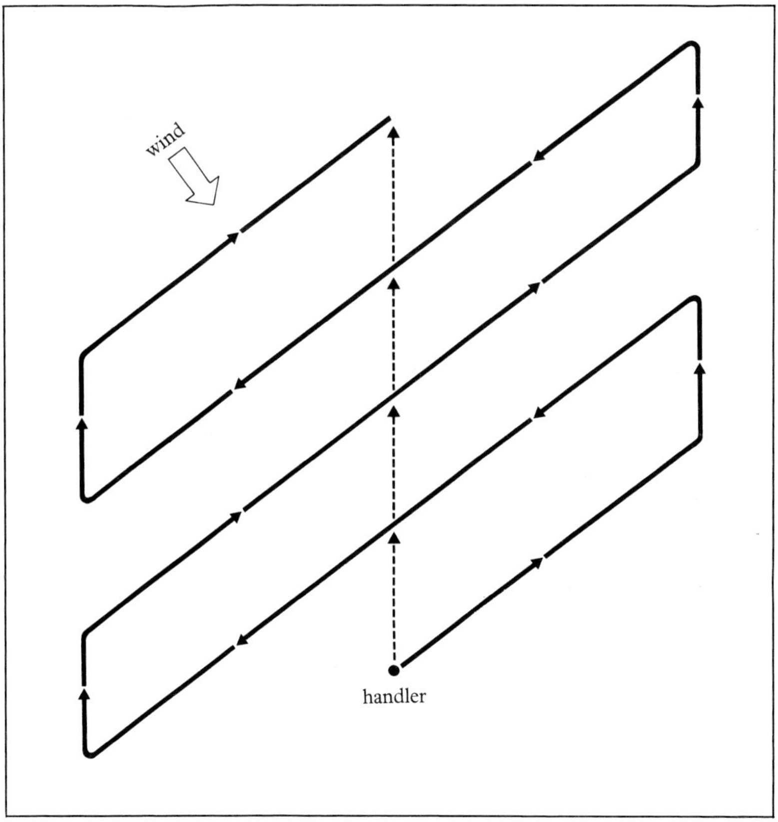

Figure 7

easily taught, although some dogs need a lot of persuasion not to move forward towards the bird when its partner is on point. Use of the command DOWN or HUP or one whistle blast or the giving of the command TO HO followed by the command WAIT (or just WAIT alone) should stop the dog when it sees its partner on point. But to back is not a reflex action to a dog trained to point its own game, and so it should be stopped and stroked to encourage it to point whenever its partner does so. The backing dog must be watched carefully to see that it remains down throughout the point, flush, shot, road and point of a dead bird. It must not move an inch whilst these manoeuvres are carried out. When this is done to perfection a dog may work in brace and give much pleasure and added coverage to the hunt.

A pointer backing

CHAPTER NINE

Special Training for Pointer-Retrievers

These dogs – all of Continental origin – are gundog geniuses. Retrievers must learn to retrieve, spaniels must learn to hunt, flush and retrieve. Pointers and setters must learn to hunt, point and flush. These retriever-pointers must learn to hunt, point, flush and retrieve. That is quite a curriculum encompassing, as it does, *all* the lessons learnt by all the other groups of gundogs.

To Ho

For the beginning of their training they need all the early lessons of the retriever (pages 95–109). When a retriever moves on to retrieving lessons the pointer-retriever parts company with that programme and starts to learn to point like a setter. These lessons are designed to produce a good point, good discipline to TO HO and a steady move on to flush and the roading out of the covey. For the method of teaching this refer to that section on setters on pages 151–162.

Quartering

Now the dog must tackle quartering and learn a method and pattern adapted to differing wind conditions. Quartering lessons should of course start on gameless ground and be restricted to 40 or 50 yards either side of the handler to start with, this distance to be extended only when the turn to the whistle is absolutely obeyed.

Drop to Flush

Next the combination of quarter and point can be connected to the drop to flush with dizzied pigeon or live birds and ground game, and this is as far as these lessons should go for the dog's first season (see pages 151–158). *A pointer-retriever should be taught to hunt, point, and flush and no more in its first season.*

It is pretty obvious that if you are going to add to these skills the accomplishments of retrieving and hunting close country to flush like a spaniel, a dog may quickly lose its staunchness to the point which is so vital if on a big moor the walking guns are to have time to get into position before the flush. These dogs are needed to perform the setter's or pointer's duties on big country where the range may be over a 300 yard front, and to do this they must absorb the staunch lessons of the moor and the stubbles. So the first season should be devoted to ranging to a tight pattern, pointing and moving forward to the flush.

This hunting must be carried out with head high and the nostrils searching across the wind for scent.

Retrieving

Now in the second season comes a transition to different disciplines demanding different body actions. The dog, steady to flush and gunfire, is now to be taught to retrieve. Retrieving entails hunting a blood scent – quite different from the scent of live game – and the hunt for a dead bird must be carried out with head down hunting the blood trail.

Retrieving principles (see pages 111–116) are taught with dummies as they are to a retriever and, once the dog has confirmed its instinct and willingness to retrieve, many of the dummies thrown should be picked by the trainer to get it fixed in the dog's mind that the firing of a gun and fall of a dummy do not signify that a retrieve will

German short-haired pointer retrieving a widgeon

always follow. This is a steadiness lesson, and it is most important that the staunchness to point that has been reinforced by a season's practice should not now be destroyed by a predilection on the part of the dog to become unsteady to the shot and fall of a dummy. *It is most important that a pointer-retriever be taught to be steady to the fall of a dummy* (see pages 111–112).

Flushing

Now comes an even more difficult transition for the dog. Already it points like a pointer and retrieves like a retriever. Now it must learn, in close country, to hunt and flush like a spaniel. Pointer-retrievers are supposed to be 'all purpose', but in my view a combination of the skills of a setter and a retriever or of a spaniel and a retriever are all that should be asked of a pointer-retriever. To learn to be staunch to the point in open country and to go straight in to the flush in closed country is to my mind asking too much of a dog, and the attempt to encompass all those skills is the reason why many gundog men are sceptical of the claims of prowess made by pointer-retriever experts. What I am saying is that the triple disciplines of staunchness to point in the open, drive into the flush in cover and steadiness to the retrieve are too much for one dog to encompass, and two such achievements will, in general, prove to be plenty enough for most samples of these undoubtedly versatile dogs.

But suppose you can train a dog to such tasks. Imagine the thrill of being able to take the dog to range and point over a 300 yard front on a grouse moor, and then up on to retrieve the shot game having sat to flush, shot and fall. Then down to the woodlands and bramble to quest back and forth on a 30 yard front like a spaniel, pushing all game out of its seat with energy and drive, steady to flush, shot and fall and then on to the retrieve. And finally sitting steady at heel during a big drive of pheasants, getting the head down to a strong runner and returning in triumph with a live bird to hand. Of course a visit to a marsh for duck flighting and long cross-water retrieves in the half-light will be taken in its stride by such a paragon of a dog, provided its trainer has been able to produce all these skills.

But do remember the difficulty of teaching a dog to stay steady to the point in the open and to move straight in to the flush in close country. It is no good getting these skills mixed up, for a quick flush on a grouse moor will result in birds in the air far away from the guns, whilst in dense cover it is irrelevant for a dog to go on point unseen by its handler. I think you should decide if you want a pointer or a spaniel and settle for perfection in one of these disciplines.

Pointer-retrievers are often taught a special method of pointing: they raise a front leg when pointing feather and a hind leg when pointing fur. It is not difficult, given the availability of live game, to teach this refinement by lifting the appropriate leg when the dog is on point, and it is a nice skill to inculcate.

Umschlangen

A useful trick of pointer-retrievers is to perform what in German is called the 'Umschlangen' which means the 'strike round'. It is the technique, once the dog is on point, of moving round the game holding its scent in its high-held nostrils, stalking with belly low to the ground and getting to the opposite side of the bird from the handler, so that at the flush the bird may be pushed over the gun. Not until every possible lesson in steadiness on the point is fully encompassed should this be taught. To do so it is necessary when the dog is on point to give it the hand signals 'go right' or 'left' and 'go straight on' so that it moves round the game. This is an instinctive movement in many pointer-retrievers and can be quickly taught. In other dogs it can cause much confusion.

The best job to my mind for these dogs is with one or two guns hunting, pointing, flushing and retrieving on a rough shooting day. They can cover so much ground and bring so much game to the gun and then retrieve it that they are the rough shooter's dog *par excellence*.

CHAPTER TEN

Field Trials

Field trials are designed to tell a gundog's working ability in conditions which as near as possible simulate an ordinary day's shooting. They are run under Kennel Club Rules and the work is judged by Judges approved by the Kennel Club.

The Kennel Club publishes 'Field Trial Rules' and a 'Guide to Field Trial Judges', and they are worth setting out because careful reading will enlighten the potential field trialler as to the object of the exercise and the method recommended for the conduct and judging of the trial.

Competitors at a field trial with their pointers awaiting the next stake

EXTRACTS FROM THE KENNEL CLUB FIELD TRIAL RULES

A Field Trial is a meeting for the purpose of holding competitions for the work of dogs in the field.

A Stake is a competition held at a Field Trial.

A Nomination is the right to enter at some subsequent date a dog to compete in a stake.

The Draw is the selection by ballot of the order in which dogs in a stake should compete.

A Prize is a money prize or prize of any description won in a stake, other than a Special Prize.

An Award of Honour is not a prize but may be awarded at the discretion of the Judges to the dog officially placed reserve in any Stake.

A Diploma of Merit is not a prize, but may be awarded at the discretion of the Judges at a Championship Meeting.

A Certificate of Merit is not a prize, but may be awarded at the discretion of the Judges in any stake.

The Breeder of any dog is the owner of the dam at the time of whelping unless a variation of this definition has been effected under the Regulations for Loan or Use of Bitch for Breeding Purposes.

An Open Stake is a Stake open to all dogs of a named breed, without restrictions as to age or residential qualification of the owner, but it may be limited to a prescribed number decided by ballot.

An All-Aged Stake is an Open Stake, but restricted by the regulations of the Society promoting the Field Trials.

The Title of Field Trial Champion

The following dogs shall be entitled to be described as Field Trial Champions:

Pointers and Setters

(i) The winner of the Pointer and Setter Championship Stake or

(ii) A dog which wins two first prizes at two different Field Trials in Open or All-Aged Stakes for Pointers and Setters in which there are no fewer than 8 runners.

One of these wins must be in a stake open to Pointers and all breeds of Setters.

Retrievers

(i) The winner of the Retriever Championship Stake or

(ii) A dog which wins two first prizes at two different Field Trials in Open or All-Aged Stakes for Retrievers. In 12-dog stakes there must be no fewer than 8 runners and in 24-dog stakes no fewer than 16 runners in order for the stakes to qualify.

One of these wins must be in a stake open to all breeds of

Retrievers. In order to qualify both stakes must be for not more than 12 nominations with one day allotted for judging and not more than 24 nominations with two days alloted for judging.

Before a Retriever is entitled to be described as a Field Trial Champion it must also have sat quietly at a drive and have passed a water test. These conditions must have been fulfilled at the Championship, in a Field Trial Stake before two Panel 'A' Judges or at a subsequent special test before two Panel 'A' Judges.

COCKER SPANIELS

(i) The winner of the Cocker Spaniel Championship Stake or

(ii) A dog which wins two first prizes at two different Field Trials in Open or All-Aged Stakes for Cocker Spaniels or open to any breed of Spaniel.

With the exception of the Spaniel Championship all Stakes must be limited to 16 dogs and not more than 16 dogs may run on any one day, irrespective of the number of Stakes. In order for the stakes to qualify there must be no fewer than 8 runners in Stakes for Cocker Spaniels and no fewer than 12 runners in Stakes open to any breed of Spaniel.

SPANIELS (OTHER THAN COCKER)

(i) The winner of the Championship Stake for Spaniels (other than Cocker) or

(ii) A dog which wins two first prizes at two different Field Trials in Open or All-Aged Stakes for Spaniels.

With the exception of the Spaniel Championship all Stakes must be limited to 16 dogs and not more than 16 dogs may run on any one day, irrespective of the number of Stakes. In order for the Stakes to qualify there must be no fewer than 12 runners in each Stake.

Before a Spaniel is entitled to be described as a Field Trial Champion it must also have satisfied the requirement of Regulation 16 (the water test) of the General Regulations for the Conduct of Field Trials. These requirements must have been fulfilled at the Championship, in a Field Trial Stake before two Panel 'A' Judges or at a subsequent special test before two Panel 'A' Judges.

BREEDS WHICH HUNT, POINT, AND RETRIEVE

A dog which wins two first prizes at two different Field Trials in Open or All-Aged Stakes in which there are no fewer than 8 runners.

One of the above wins must be in a Stake open to all breeds which hunt, point and retrieve.

General Regulations for the Conduct of Field Trials

DEFINITIONS

(i) A Puppy is a dog whelped not earlier than the 1st January in the year preceding the date of the Field Trials, but in any stake run in January a dog which was a puppy in the previous month shall be deemed to be a puppy.

(ii) Novice or Non-Winners Stakes for Spaniels, unless otherwise stated, are confined to dogs which have not won a First Prize other than in Puppy, Brace or Team Stakes prior to the closing of entries.

(iii) A Brace Stake is a stake for two dogs of the same breed entered as a Brace by the same owner.

(iv) A Team Stake is a stake for three or more dogs of the same breed entered as a Team by the same owner.

1 (a) THE SCHEDULE. A Society holding a Field Trial must issue a Schedule which is to be treated as a contract between the Society and the public. No modifications may be made except by permission of the Kennel Club, followed by advertisement in suitable papers if time permits before the closing of entries. The Secretary of the Society shall send a copy of the Schedule to the Kennel Club within 3 days of printing. The Schedule must contain:

(i) The date and place of the Field Trial, and number of nominations accepted.

(ii) The latest date for applying for a nomination if such is required.

(iii) The latest date for receiving entries.

(iv) The amounts of nomination and/or entry fees and of prize money.

(v) The conditions for the Draw and for intimating acceptance or refusal of a nomination.

(vi) A statement that the Field Trial is held under Kennel Club Field Trial Rules and Regulations.

(vii) A definition of any Stake not defined in these Rules, or Regulations.

(viii) The names of the Judges, where possible.

(ix) The order in which the Stakes will be run.

(x) A statement of the proportion of entry fee to be returned to entrants should any stake have to be abandoned owing to the weather being unfit.

(xi) For Retrievers and Spaniels, if the Trial includes an Open or All-Aged Stake, an indication of whether that Stake carries a qualification for the Championship.

1 (b) THE CARD. A Society holding a Field Trial must publish a Card which must contain:

On the front outside cover

(i) The name of the Society.
(ii) The breed(s) for which Stakes are run at the Trial.
(iii) Date(s) of the Trial.
(iv) For Retrievers and Spaniels, if the Trial includes an Open or All-Aged Stake, an indication of whether that Stake carries a qualification for the Championship.
(v) Names of the Judges.
(vi) Venue of the Trial.

Contents

(i) A definition of each State to be run in the Trial.
(ii) The Prizes offered.
(iii) Entries listed in numerical order as follows:
Registered name of dog.
Name of owner.
Breed of dog.
Sex of dog.
Date of birth.
Registered names of sire and dam.
Name of breeder.
Name of handler.
(iv) A list of the names and addresses of owners of all dogs in the Trial in alphabetical order.
The Secretary of the Society shall send to the Kennel Club within one week of the meeting a copy of the card with all awards marked thereon.
(v) A statement that the Trial is held under Kennel Club Field Trial Rules and Regulations.
(vi) A statement that the Society accepts no responsibility for injury, loss or damage to person or property however occasioned.

2. Copy of Rules. The Secretary of the Society shall send a copy of these Rules to any applicant and shall have a copy with him or his representative on the ground during a meeting.

3. Awards. Equal awards for any of the prizes offered at a Field Trial are prohibited.

4. Record of Entries. The Secretary shall preserve all entry forms for six months after the meeting, and produce any of them to any official body inquiring into an objection or dispute.

5. Appointment of Judges. The Judges shall be appointed by the Society. The General Committee shall issue to Field Trial Societies Panels of Judges for Field Trials for Retrievers, Spaniels, Pointers and Setters, and breeds which hunt, point and retrieve. Before a Judge can be considered for addition to any panel he must be recommended by a Field Trial Society for which he has judged. The qualifications required before a Judge can be added to a panel are:

Panel A. *Retrievers and Spaniels*
Before a Judge can be added to this panel he must have judged at least two Open Stakes and two other Stakes run under Kennel Club Field Trial Rules and Regulations and held by two different Societies registered with the Kennel Club.

Panel A. *Pointers and Setters*
Before a Judge can be added to this panel he must have judged at least two Stakes.

Panel A. *Breeds which hunt, point and retrieve*
Before a Judge can be added to this panel he must have judged at least two Stakes, one of which must be an Open Stake.

Panel B. *Retrievers and Spaniels*
Before a Judge can be added to this panel he must have judged at least two Stakes.

Panel B. *Pointers and Setters*
Before a Judge can be added to this panel he must have judged at least one Stake.

Panel B. *Breeds which hunt, point and retrieve*
Before a Judge can be added to this panel he must have judged at least two Stakes.

The compulsory number of Panel A Judges for the various Stakes is as follows:

	Retrievers	*Spaniels*	*Pointers and Setters*	*Breeds which hunt, point and retrieve*
Championship	All A	All A	All A	—
Open and All-Aged Stakes	2 A	1 A	1 A	1 A
Non-Winner and other Stakes	1 A	1 A	1 A	1 A

The General Committee shall have power to add names to the panels from time to time and also to remove names at their discretion. The General Committee may at its discretion take into account the experience of Judges at Field Trials held under the Irish Kennel Club Field Trial Rules and Regulations when considering the addition of names to the Panels.

When there are four Judges for a Stake they must judge in pairs, each pair watching the work jointly of one dog at the same time. Each pair of Judges must decide between themselves which of them is to give the commands.

If only two of the four Judges are on Panel A they must not judge together but must each take one of the Judges not on Panel A as their co-Judge.

No Judge shall shoot at a Field Trial at which he is judging.

The Secretary of a Field Trial must include a copy of the 'Guide to Field Trial Judges R (3)', issued by the Kennel Club Field Trials Committee, in the judge's book.

6. NOMINATIONS. A nomination is the right to enter at some future date a dog owned and registered at the Kennel Club in the name of the applicant for the nomination. If a partnership of two or more persons make application for a nomination for the partnership, then only one of the partners shall be permitted to apply for a separate nomination for a dog registered at the Kennel Club in his sole ownership. If applications exceed the number of nominations available, the right to a nomination shall be decided by ballot. If a nomination be not returned to the Secretary of the Society by a date specified in the Schedule the applicant will be held to have accepted it and be liable for the full entry fee, unless the Secretary can transfer the nomination to some other applicant.

7. REDUCING PRIZE MONEY. If the full number of nominations be not applied for or nominations not accepted cannot be transferred

to other applicants, the prizes may be reduced at the option of the society.

The amount of prize money offered by a Society may be made to depend on the number of entries received.

8. ORDER OF RUNNING. The draw shall take place at such time and in such conditions as are stated in the Schedule, and at it each dog must be given the number that accords with its place in the draw, and every dog must be tried in order of draw.

9. MANAGEMENT AT FIELD TRIALS. The management of a Field Trial shall be entrusted to the Society, who shall decide any disputed question by a majority of those present.

Secretaries of Field Trials must ensure that a handler and dog are always available to pick up wounded game when required.

10. WEATHER CONDITIONS. If the Society considers the weather unfit for holding the Trial, the stake or stakes may be cancelled and a proportion of the entry fees decided by the Society and published in the Schedule, shall be returned to entrants, or a fresh draw may be made and a fresh date fixed for the abandoned stake or stakes.

11. HANDLING OF DOGS. If a deputy handles a dog, the owner may be in the line but must take no part in the working of the dog. All handlers must obey the orders of the Judges. Handlers will not be allowed to carry in their hand gun, stick, whip, shooting stick, or lead, whilst handling their dogs, but in cases of physical disability a shooting stick may be carried with the permission of the Judges. A Spaniel Society may, however, hold a Special Stake in which it is compulsory for all handlers to shoot over their dogs.

No handler may handle more than 3 dogs in any single dog Stake for Retrievers or Spaniels, or more than 5 dogs in any single dog Stake for Pointers and Setters.

When there are four Judges at a Retriever Trial there is no objection to relatives of the Judges running dogs. When called up by the judges, a handler may wear only the armband relevant to the dogs being judged.

12. DOGS UNDER TRIAL. The control of all matters connected with dogs under trial shall rest with the Judges of the meeting, but they may call the Secretary to their assistance if they think fit.

The Judges are empowered to turn out of the Stake any dog

whose handler does not obey them, or wilfully interferes with another competitor or his dog.

13. PHYSICAL CONDITION. Should the members of the Committee present, after consultation with the Judges, consider a dog is unfit to compete by reason of sexual causes or of any contagious disease or from an attack of hysteria occurring on the ground or any other cause which interferes with the safety or chance of winning of his opponents, such dog must be removed immediately from the ground and from the Trials. Any such case is liable to be reported to the Kennel Club and dealt with under Rules 13 or 14.

If a dog competes which has been exposed to the risk of any contagious or infectious disease during the period of six weeks prior to the Field Trial and/or if any dog shall be proved to be suffering at a Field Trial from any contagious of infectious disease, including contagious results of inoculations against distemper, the owner thereof shall be liable to be dealt with under Rule 13.

14. UNPUNCTUALITY. A dog which is not present when required by a Judge may be disqualified.

15. DISCARDING DOGS. No dog shall be discarded until it has been tried by two Judges except that it shall be discarded if it has run in or chased or refused to enter water or if two Judges concur that the dog is out of control of his handler or is held to have a hard mouth; but all the Judges must have examined the injured game before the dog is discarded for hard mouth.

The handler should be given the opportunity of examining the damaged game in the presence of the judges, but the decision of the Judges is final.

A dog which whines or barks in the opinion of a Judge shall be discarded from the Stake.

In the Retriever Championship Stake the discarding of dogs shall be entirely at the discretion of the Judges.

16. WATER TEST. A Water Test requires a dog to enter water readily and swim to the satisfaction of the judges. In Retriever and Spaniel Stakes and Stakes for breeds which hunt, point and retrieve, a dog which fails a Water Test shall not receive an award in that Stake. If a Water Test is held, all dogs placed in the awards must have passed this test. A handler is not entitled to ask for a shot to be fired. A Special Water Test conducted in accordance with the pro-

visions of Field Trial Rule 9 – Title of Field Trial Champion must be held between 1st October and 1st February.

17. Awards of Honour, Diplomas of Merit and Certificates of Merit. Judges shall be empowered to award Diplomas of Merit in Championship Stakes and Certificates of Merit in all other Stakes to those dogs, apart from the prize winners, which have, in their opinion acquitted themselves sufficiently well to warrant them.

A dog officially placed Reserve shall receive an Award of Honour or a Certificate of Merit at the discretion of the Judges. At a Championship meeting a dog officially placed Reserve shall receive an Award of Honour or a Diploma of Merit at the discretion of the Judges.

18. Withholding Prizes. The Judges are empowered and instructed to withhold any prize or award if, in their opinion, the dogs competing do not show sufficient merit.

19. Withdrawal of Dogs. No dog entered for competition and once under a Judge at the Trial may be withdrawn from competition without the consent of the Society.

No competitor may leave the field without the permission of the Judges or Society and any dog so removed is liable to disqualification.

20. Impugning Decisions. Anyone taking part in a Trial openly impugning the decision of the Judge or Judges shall render himself liable to be reported to the Field Trials Committee of the Kennel Club under the provisions of Kennel Club Field Trial Rule No. 13.

KENNEL CLUB GUIDE TO FIELD TRIAL JUDGES

These notes are designed to assist Judges in selecting the best shooting dogs. They are not intended to be rules, as these have already been laid down by the Kennel Club. The Field Trial Rules and Regulations and also the Field Trial Council recommendations, approved by the Kennel Club Field Trials Committee, can be obtained from the Kennel Club.

No Judge should accept an invitation to judge Trials unless he is fully conversant with these Rules and Regulations and has studied the Guide to Field Trial Judges.

The Secretary of a Field Trial should ensure that each of the Judges at a Field Trial has a copy of this Guide.

Retrievers

1. At the start of a Field Trial, Judges should make sure that they have the correct dogs in the line, lowest number on the right.

2. Judges should take gamefinding to be of the first importance in Field Trials.

3. Judges at Open Retriever Stakes are advised to ask their Guns not to shoot directly over a dog when it is out working. In Puppy, Novice and Non-Winner Stakes, Judges are advised to ask their Guns not to shoot when a dog is out working.

4. All wounded game must be gathered as expeditiously as possible and must be killed at the earliest opportunity. Wounded game must be recovered before dead game. If a Judge cannot gather wounded game, he must be careful to depute this task to the official handler and dog appointed for this purpose.

5. If a bird is shot very close to a dog which would make the retrieve of no value, the Judge should pick the bird by hand or offer it to another Judge. During the first round of the Stake, dogs should have the opportunity on game shot by their own guns.

6. After all the dogs have been tried once, Judges may call up for trial any dog at their discretion.

7. Judges should be most careful to see that each dog gets its chance in the correct order, starting with the lowest number on the right. Should dog No. 1 fail, and dog No. 2 be successful, No. 2 still has the first chance in the next retrieve. It is quite unfair to give a dog two first chances in succession and the other dog two second chances. If the two dogs fail on a bird, the Judge should not call fresh dogs into the line to try for the bird until dogs already in the line have been tried. In the concluding stages of a Trial, Judges may use their own discretion as the situation arises.

8. In the first round of a Stake, if the amount of game permits, a dog should have a minimum of two opportunities to retrieve before

the next dog is called up, but the actual number of retrieves is at the discretion of the Judges according to the merit of the work done.

9. When a number of dogs have been tried and have failed on a bird, the Judge should not look for it unless all the Judges agree that no more dogs should be tried. Once Judges have looked for and found a bird, no more dogs should be tried on it.

10. Handlers should be instructed where to try from and given reasonable directions as to where the game fell.

11. Good marking is essential in a Retriever as he should not disturb game unnecessarily. Judges should give full credit to a dog which goes straight to the fall and gets on with the job.

12. At a drive, the placings of the dogs shall be at the discretion of the Judge with the lowest number on the right. The Kennel Club Field Trial Rules state that a dog which whines or barks in the opinion of a Judge shall be discarded from the Stake.

13. A dog must walk steadily to heel.

14. The perfect pick up should be quick with a fast return. The handler should not snatch or drag the game from the dog's mouth. Judges should not penalise a dog too heavily for putting a bird down to get a firmer grip, but this must not, however, be confused with sloppy retrieving. A good gamefinding dog should not rely on the handler to find the bird. He should, however, be obedient and respond to this handler's signals when necessary. Dogs showing gamefinding ability and initiative should be placed above those which have to be handled on to their game. Usually, the best dog seems to require the least handling. He appears to have an instinctive knowledge of direction and makes difficult finds look simple and easy. Steadiness to fur is most important and, where possible, dogs should be given fur to retrieve.

15. If a dog is performing indifferently on a runner, it should be called up promptly. If three or more dogs are tried on a runner, the work of all these dogs must be assessed in relation to the order in which they are tried.

16. If a bird is known to have run, the handlers of the second and subsequent dogs down should be allowed to take their dogs towards

the fall, and the first dog also if he has not had a chance to mark the bird.

17. A dog which has its eye wiped on a dead bird should be penalised, but all eye-wipes should be treated on their merits.

If a dog shows ability by acknowledging the fall and making a workmanlike job of the line, it should not automatically be barred from the prize list by failing to produce the bird providing that the bird is not collected by another dog tried by the Judges on the same bird.

18. All game should be examined for signs of 'hard mouth'. A hard-mouthed dog seldom gives visible evidence of hardness. He will simply crush in one or both sides of the ribs. Blowing up the feathers will not disclose the damage. Place the bird on the palm of the hand, breast upwards, head forward, and feel the ribs with finger and thumb. They should be round and firm. If they are caved in or flat, this is definite evidence of hard mouth. Be sure the bird reaches your co-Judges for examination. There should be no hesitation or sentiment with 'hard mouth' – the dog should be discarded. A certain indication of a good mouth is a dog bringing in a live bird whose head is up and eye bright. Superficial damage, if any, in this case can be ignored. At times, the rump of a strong runner may be gashed and look ugly. Care should be taken here, as it may be the result of a difficult capture or lack of experience in mastering a strong runner by a young dog. Judges should always satisfy themselves that any damage done has been caused by the dog, not by the shot or fall, and in cases of doubt, the benefit should be given to the dog. Handlers should be given the opportunity of inspecting the damaged game in the presence of the Judges, but the decision of the Judges is final.

19. If more than one bird is down and the dog changes birds on his way back he should be severely penalised.

20. The standard of work in Stakes carrying Field Trial Championship status should be higher than in Novice, Non-Winner and Puppy Stakes, where more leniency is allowed.

21. Judges should keep their opinions strictly to themselves and act on what happens on the day or days of the Trials at which they are judging, forgetting past performances at previous Trials.

22. Judges are advised to place each dog in a category such as A, B and C, according to the work done at the end of each round.

23. In the concluding stages of a Trial, the dogs should all be in the centre under all the Judges.

24. It is advisable to take short notes of each dog's work and not to trust to memory.

25. It is in the interests of all Field Trial supporters that Judges should be as courteous and co-operative as possible with the Host and Steward of the Beat and fall in with their arrangements. This goes a long way towards making a success of the Trial and the possibility of receiving an invitation for another year.

26. Summary of points

ELIMINATING FAULTS: Hard mouth · Whining or barking · Running in and chasing · Out of control · Failing to enter water.

MAJOR FAULTS: Failing to find game · Unsteadiness at heel · Eye wipe · Disturbing ground · Slack and unbusinesslike work · Noisy handling · Poor control · Changing birds.

CREDIT POINTS: Natural gamefinding ability · Nose · Marking ability · Drive · Style · Quickness in gathering game · Control · Quietness in handling · Retrieving and delivery.

Spaniels

NOTE. The attention of Judges is particularly drawn to paragraph 11 of this section which deals with the duties of a Referee.

1. Before starting a Trial, Judges should ask the Steward of the Beat what the game position is likely to be and regulate the number of retrieves to each dog accordingly. They should also satisfy themselves that arrangements have been made for the collection of dead or wounded game which they do not require.

2. A Field Trial should be run as nearly as possible to an ordinary day's shooting, and artificial retrieves should be restricted to a minimum.

3. A Spaniel should at all times work in range with good treatment of ground; under no circumstances should it pass over game on the beat it is working. A Spaniel's first job is to find game and flush

within range of the gun. The direction of the wind has a considerable influence on the way a dog will work ground. With a head-on wind, the dog should quarter the ground systematically left to right and vice versa, making good all likely game-holding cover, but keeping within gunshot distance of the handler. With a following wind it will be very different. The dog will often want to pull well out, then work back towards the handler. Judges should regulate the pace of the line to allow the dog to do this and make good his ground. Often a dog has been penalised for missing game when, in fact, the line has been moving forward too fast to permit the dog to make good the ground. Lines and foot scents should be ignored. Persistent 'pulling on' on foot scents is annoying and unprofitable, resulting in game being missed. During this period, the Judge can assess the gamefinding ability and nose of the dog, also pace, drive, treatment of ground, and possibly courage.

4. A dog which catches un-shot game should be discarded unless in the opinion of the Judges there are extenuating circumstances. Should a dog indicate or strike at game without effect, the handler may 'stop' his dog and appeal to the Judges for permission to flush the game.

5. If a dog points or hesitates slightly before flushing, this is an added refinement, but the dog must flush on command.

6. A dog should 'stop' to game and shot automatically, but if a dog moves a little in order to make the fall, if this is obscured, this shows intelligence and should be credited. For instance, in thick cover, a dog should push game into the open and check after doing so.

7. Good marking should always be looked for and given full credit, and bad marking penalised.

If a dog shows ability by acknowledging the fall and making a workmanlike job of the line, it should not automatically be barred from the prize list by failing to produce the bird providing that the bird is not collected by another dog tried by the judges on the same bird.

8. A Spaniel should pick up cleanly, return quickly and deliver well up to hand. Such a retrieve is desirable, but too much should not be made of a momentary check, particularly through cover, as the dog may have had a long gruelling hunt up to the time of flushing and thus making the retrieve possible and this should be allowed for.

On no occasion should a dog be sent on a long, blind retrieve, but should be taken to within a reasonable distance of the fall, bearing conditions in mind. Normally, it is unwise to try more than two dogs on one retrieve.

9. All game should be examined for signs of 'hard mouth'. A hard-mouthed dog seldom gives visible evidence of hardness. He will simply crush in one or both sides of the bird. Blowing up the feathers will not disclose the damage. Place the bird on the palm of the hand, breast upwards, head forward, and feel the ribs with finger and thumb. They should be round and firm. If they are caved in or flat, this is definite evidence of hard mouth. Be sure the bird reaches your co-Judges for examination. There should be no hesitation or sentiment with 'hard mouth' – the dog should be discarded. A certain indication of a good mouth is a dog bringing in a live bird whose head is up and eye bright. Superficial damage, if any, in this case can be ignored. At times, the rump of a strong runner may be gashed and look ugly. Care should be taken here, as it may be the result of a difficult capture or lack of experience in mastering a strong runner by a young dog. Judges should always satisfy themselves that any damage done has been caused by the dog, not by the shot or fall, and, in cases of doubt, the benefit should be given to the dog. Handlers should be given the opportunity of inspecting the damaged game in the presence of the Judges but the decision of the Judges is final.

10. A dog should have drive and thrust and face cover well, and, at the same time, should be amenable and gay, in short, a pleasure to watch. It should show good treatment of ground with the minimum of help from its handler. All things being equal, the stylish dog should be given the credit. Judges should, however, be satisfied that the fast stylish dog is also the best gamefinder.

11. A Referee should not take any part whatever in the judging of a Stake unless the Judges appeal to him to settle a point or an award on which they cannot agree, but he should make notes on the work of the dogs. When a dog has been under two Judges and they both agree, and feel certain that this is their best dog, they are quite in order in putting it on one side and running off for the remaining places.

12. Judges are advised to place each dog in a category such as A, B and C according to the work done at the end of each run, and

usually they will find little difficulty in getting down to the placings. With dogs of equal merit, they can be divided by running them side by side. The main consideration should now be style, pace, ground treatment, and the dog's response to the handler. Judges should walk side by side, but not encroach on each other's beats.

13. A Judge should refrain from talking to anyone while the dog is actively competing under him. From the moment the dog starts questing, he should make every effort to keep that dog in view and so place himself, when the dog is sent out for a retrieve, to enable him to observe every move of the dog until the game is delivered to hand.

14. It is advisable to take short notes of each dog's work and not to trust to memory.

15. Summary of points
ELIMINATING FAULTS: Hard mouth · Whining or Barking · Running in and chasing · Out of control · Failing to enter water · Deliberately catching unwounded game (Elimination for this fault is at the Judges' discretion.)
MAJOR FAULTS: Failing to find game · Not quartering and not making ground good · Not stopping to shot and game · Disturbing ground · Noisy handling · Poor control.
CREDIT POINTS: Natural gamefinding ability · Nose · Drive · Marking ability · Style · Control · Quickness in gathering game · Quietness in handling · Retrieving and delivery.

Pointers and Setters

1. The task of Judges is to find the dog which, on the day, pleases them most by the quality of its work from the shooting point of view.

2. It is the duty of Judges to give the dogs every opportunity to work well by seeing that conditions are in their favour as far as possible, and also, where feasible, to demonstrate to competitors and spectators how their decisions are reached. It is the better dogs who should be fully tried and not the hopeless ones.

3. The first round, having been drawn in accordance with the rules, should be proceeded with as rapidly as possible. Each brace, except in cases of undoubted lack of merit, should be tried for at least 15

minutes. 'Undoubted lack of merit' is behaviour which convinces the Judges that no Certificate of Merit can be awarded to the dog concerned. When this has been confirmed by consultation between the Judges, the brace should be picked up, or a bye dog, if available, tried with the survivor.

4. Stickiness on point should be severely penalised.

5. If a dog deliberately gallops into game up wind, he should be discarded, but if, on the other hand, he is coming down wind and drops immediately the birds rise, this does not constitute a flush. Chasing live game, be it fur or feather, must put a dog out of the Stake.

6. Dogs should be penalised if they do not drop to shot.

7. Judges should appreciate that different breeds have different styles of working, and should make themselves conversant with these styles.

8. Persistent false point should be severely penalised.

9. Full credit should be given to a dog which backs naturally.

10. Noisy handling should be penalised.

11. Finding the winner should consist of taking into consideration the whole quality of the dog's work, not just the number of points he has made. Gamefinding, of course, is essential, but the dog's whole method of working should be a pleasure to watch, such as quartering his ground methodically, and making it all good, natural backing, steadiness and style on point, and pace. Though the Trial should not be run as a 'knock-out' competition, it is desirable, if possible, that the winner should have run against the second and the third against the fourth. Otherwise, variation in the conditions of scent and presence of game make too great a difference in the results and tend to over-emphasise the luck of the draw.

12. Judges should exercise considerable control over the proceedings and endeavour to get the dogs running in favourable wind. They should also conserve the ground by being as decisive as possible.

13. Judges should keep up with the handlers and try to see everything that takes place at a Trial. Frequently, a Judge is two or three

hundred yards behind and is unable to see all the work. This does not mean that he should try and keep up with a dog that is obviously running out of his ground.

14. It is advisable to take short notes of each dog's work and not to trust to memory.

15. Judges are advised to place each dog in a category such as A, B and C, according to the work done at the end of each round.

16. Summary of points
ELIMINATING FAULTS: Flushing up wind · Out of control · Chasing fur or feather.
MAJOR FAULTS: Not quartering and not making ground good · Not dropping to shot · Stickiness on point · Not dropping to flush down wind · Missing birds.
CREDIT POINTS: Game finding · Natural backing · Style on point · Pace · Quartering.

Breeds which Hunt, Point and Retrieve

1. Trials should be run as nearly as possible to an ordinary day's shooting. Judges are responsible for the proper conduct of the Trial in accordance with Kennel Club Regulations and with the Schedule for the Stake. They should co-operate with the Host and the Steward of the Beat to achieve the best result in an atmosphere of friendliness and confidence. If conditions force them to depart from usual practice they should explain the reasons to handlers and spectators. Guns and handlers should be briefed at the start.

2. Judges at Open and All-Aged Stakes should ask the guns to shoot everything, except directly over a dog out working. In other stakes Judges should ask the guns to shoot only over the 'point' and when the handler is beside his dog, unless otherwise directed.

3. The first round should be taken as drawn. For subsequent rounds Judges may call forward dogs at their discretion, so that those showing merit will be thoroughly tested and given every opportunity in roughly comparable conditions of wind, scent and ground. Dogs which are not forward within 15 minutes of being called may be disqualified.

4. Judges should so position themselves that they can see every move of the dogs while in the line. They should regulate the pace of

the line to the handler and dog to avoid game being flushed on a part of the beat not yet covered by the dog. Game so flushed should not be counted as missed by the dog.

5. Judges should accede to a request from the handler of a puppy in a Novice or Puppy stake who asks to be excused from retrieving fur.

6. If a dog catches game and the judges are satisfied that the game was unwounded and undamaged, the dog should be eliminated. When it appears that game will not flush for the dog, the handler may ask permission to take up his dog, and should only be marked down for handling if subsequently shown to have been wrong.

7. Judges must confirm the arrangements for the collection of unretrieved and unwanted game.

8. Judges may discuss situations that arise and must agree the categories to be marked, but must not discuss the actual marks they award as these represent their opinions and should be kept strictly to themselves. The marks should represent the work seen on the day, and should not be influenced by past performances.

9. The standard of work in Open and All-Aged stakes carrying Field Trial Championship status should be higher than for other stakes. A prize should not be awarded unless the dog has had a productive point, a retrieve in the field and has completed the water retrieve, whatever the conditions of the day. Other stakes may be judged more leniently, but a prize should not be given unless the dog has proved himself a pointer, and a retriever on land or at the water, and has swum. Certificates of Merit are not prizes and may be awarded at the Judge's discretion to dogs showing all round qualities and that they swim.

10. Judges should mark the following categories:

(i) GROUND TREATMENT. The dog has to hunt the beat allotted thoroughly, making good all ground, missing no game and using the wind correctly. A dog that deliberately runs into game up wind should be discarded, but if he drops to birds rising down wind of him, this is a credit.

(ii) POINTING. The dog should point game staunchly, and work out only on word of command. He must be steady to flush, shot and fall. Persistent false pointing should be severely penalised, but an unproductive point, where the dog indicated by nose down and wagging tail where departed game lay should not be marked, but may be credited as a 'point' for the award of Certificate of Merit. It is accepted that hares and rabbits in their forms may not give off scent for the dog to point. Judges should not penalise dogs for failing to point in such conditions.

(iii) RETRIEVE. The retrieve must be on command. If game is shot over the point, and is marked, the dog should go straight to the fall, and any diversion marked down. With blind retrieves, Judges should indicate to the handler where the game fell. The dog should go directly as indicated by the handler and any diversion from that line, with consequent waste of time and risk of disturbance of game, should be marked down. On a long blind retrieve, the dog should be taken towards the fall. A handler should be allowed to position himself where he can see to direct the dog according to conditions, but he should be beside the Judges for the delivery.

In the case of a strong runner, the Judge should give the immediate order for a dog to be sent. Wounded game should be retrieved before dead game. The seen dead game lying in the open does not really test a good dog, should not be highly marked, and should be avoided except in stakes other than Open and All-Aged. Not more than two dogs should be tried on the same bird. When a judge goes forward to locate the game, no further dog should be tried on it. If more than one bird is down, and the dog changes birds on the way back, he should be severely marked down.

The pick up should be clean with a quick return and delivery to hand. A dog that puts game down to take a firmer grip should not be severely marked down as he may have had a gruelling stint quartering, but sloppy retrieving and finishing should be penalised.

All game should be examined for hard mouth. A hard-mouthed dog seldom gives evidence of hardness. He will simply crush in one or both sides of the bird. Blowing up the feathers will not disclose the damage. Place the bird on the palm of the hand, head forward, and feel the ribs with the finger and thumb. They should be round and firm. If they are caved in or flat, this is definite evidence of hard mouth. Be sure the bird reaches your co-Judge and the handler for examination. There should be no hesitation or sentiment with 'hard mouth' – the dog should be eliminated. A certain indication of a good mouth is a dog bringing in a live bird whose head is up and eye bright. Superficial damage, if any, in this case can be ignored. At times the rump of a strong runner may be gashed and look ugly. Care should be taken here, as it may be the result of a difficult capture, or lack of experience in mastering a strong runner by a young dog. Judges should always satisfy themselves that any damage done has been caused by the dog, not by the shot or fall, and in cases of doubt the benefit should be given to the dog. Handlers should be given the opportunity of inspecting the damaged game in the presence of the Judges, but the decision of the Judges is final.

(iv) GAME FINDING ABILITY. This is one of the highest importance. The Judges will be looking for it throughout the dog's work by the manner in which he works his beat, finds his game and responds to scent generally, and by the degree of sense of purpose and drive that he displays.

(v) STEADINESS. The dog must in all cases be steady to flush, shot and fall. He may move to mark the fall, and this may be a credit. A dog that runs in to retrieve and is stopped, and then retrieves on command, should be marked down according to the extent of the break, but the dog that does not stop should be eliminated. Dogs should be steady to fur and feather going away.

(vi) FACING COVER. There are occasions, e.g. on a grouse moor, when this category cannot be marked. Unless all dogs can be marked, none should be. In general the dog should go boldly into reasonable cover when ordered, either to push out game or to retrieve it. The Judges should agree what is reasonable.

(vii) STYLE. This embraces grace of movement, stylishness on point and on the retrieve, and the general appearance of keenness, competence and happiness in what he is doing.

(viii) HANDLING. Noisy, ineffective and over handling should be severely marked down. Usually the best dogs seem to require the least handling, but the dog should be responsive to his handler's signals.

(ix) WATER RETRIEVE. This should be fully assessed, with special attention to direct, courageous but not suicidal entry, strong swimming, direct emergence and speedy delivery to hand.

In Open and All-Aged Stakes the water retrieve is blind across water, and should be judged accordingly, including the re-entry into water carrying game.

ELIMINATIONS: Whining or barking, out of control, chasing;

failure to hunt, point, retrieve, enter water and swim, face cover; hard mouth; deliberately catching unwounded game (myxamatosis rabbits excluded).

MAJOR FAULTS: Not making ground good, missing birds, unsteadiness, stickiness on point, not acknowledging game going away, failing to find game, disturbing ground, sloppy work, noisy handling, changing birds.

CREDITS: Gamefinding ability, style on point, drive, good marking, speed and efficiency in gathering game, good water work, quiet handling.

FIELD TRIALLING

The first field trials were for pointers and setters and took place in 1865 at Southill near Bedford on Mr W. H. Whitbread's estate. The first three places were filled by Gordon setters.

It was not until 1899 that trials were held for retrieving, when spaniels and retrievers ran against one another at Mr William Arkwright's estate at Sutton Scarsdale. This was the Arkwright who seven years later was to publish the still famous book *The Pointer and his Predecessors*.

Later in that same year, 1899, at Rev B. B. Warwick's estate at Little Green, Havant, was held the first trial for retrieving dogs. The entries were: 1 Irish water spaniel, 2 clumber spaniels, 1 field spaniel, 1 curly coated retriever and 5 flatcoats. In 1902 all the entries were flatcoats. In 1904 the International Gundog League held a stake of 19 competitors: 1 Labrador, 1 curly coated retriever and 17 flatcoats. That one Labrador was an important dog. It was Munden Single owned by Mr Holland-Hibbert (later Lord Knutsford) and it won a certificate of merit, the first ever award earned by a Labrador at a trial. Major Portal's Flapper was second in the International Gundog League's trial in 1906, and in 1907 Flapper was first in the Kennel Club's All-Aged Stake.

These first Labrador wins were the initial trickle in a flood tide of success that swept the hitherto all conquering flatcoat into near oblivion. No other retriever has stood up to the Labradors. The flatcoats won once more, an inter-bred twice and goldens three times; otherwise the Labrador reigns supreme. Since the Labrador was used in the manufacture of both the flatcoat and the golden it is perhaps only just that it should emerge as the best retriever of all.

Pointer and setter trials are still held, some in the spring and the bulk in the summer in the three weeks prior to August 12th.

The Guide to Field Trial Judges sets out very clearly what is to be looked for and tested in a bird-dog. What cannot be tolerated is boring forward into the wind to flush birds – 'flushing up wind' – instead of a steady quartering patrol across the wind, running out of control or chasing. These are eliminating faults. Major faults are all due to a lack of training resulting in bad quartering, unsteadiness to shot and flush, stickiness to point – and of course missing birds. The object of pointing and setting work is to bring all game on the beat to the gun, and therefore good points include gamefinding, pace, quartering, backing and style on point.

At these trials dogs come before the Judges a brace at a time and, for the first run, work for about 15 minutes. Dogs are distinguished for the Judges' sake by differing coloured collars, usually red and white. Handlers must give great consideration to their fellow competitor and not move up wind into his unhunted ground, not steal his points, not produce so much noise and instruction as to confuse the second dog and be helpful when their own dog is about to point by telling their opposite number.

These trials are attended by real enthusiasts who, despite their lack of opportunity to work their dogs frequently in shooting situations, manage to keep pointers and setters fixed in their natural role of gameseeking in wide places.

Field Trials for spaniels are still very strong. The all-conquering spaniel today is the English springer, but cockers hold their own in the hands of one or two experts. The other breeds hardly register at all. A spaniel trial should ideally take place on rough ground, not heavily populated by game and likely to produce great variety so that pheasant, partridge, hare, rabbit, woodcock or snipe may be pushed out. This is typical rough shooting and what a spaniel is bred for. Some trials, it being difficult to get ground, take place in coverts holding reared pheasants, and although this may be better than nothing these conditions do not provide typical spaniel work especially as the birds may be around in plenty and bunched together whereas a spaniel's specialised job is to seek out scarce game. Spaniel Trials do take place in conditions similar to those encountered by a rough shooting man, and whilst many shooting men treat retriever trials with disdain there is no doubt that spaniel trials are directly responsible for keeping up the high standard of working spaniel that exists today.

There are two Judges at a spaniel trial each with two guns, and to start with the right-hand Judge takes the odd numbered dogs starting with No. 1 and the left-hand Judge the even numbers.

Casting out a spaniel at a field trial

There should also be a referee who should watch all the work of all the dogs but make no comment unless the Judges cannot agree on a point or an award and refer the matter to him.

The dogs are thus worked in pairs and are expected to hunt up all the cover on their beat whether containing game or not and to go at it with style and vigour. They should drop to flush and shot, mark the fall, go straight out to retrieve and come back with the game. Unfortunately all does not go as well as this; the bird may be a runner, or it may be impossible to mark the fall. In the first case the dog must puzzle out the line by itself for the handler will have no better knowledge of the bird's whereabouts. In the second case the handler must direct the dog by whistle and hand signal to the area of the fall. A spaniel trial is pre-eminently designed to test a dog's hunting ability, but good retrieving is also a requirement, and so on runners and unmarked birds the Judges have to bring to bear a set of rules. If the bird is not found by the first dog its bracemate should be sent for it, and if it is successful it is upgraded; but this eye-wipe should not outweigh bad hunting. If both dogs fail the Judges go forward to seek the bird themselves. If they find the bird both dogs must be eliminated. If the bird is not found the first dog is downgraded but not the second dog to try. If a dog is unsuccessful on a never-picked runner it should get credit if it takes and works a good line. This failure should not eliminate the dog; however, it should prevent it from winning this stake, though not from getting a place.

Handlers may give instructions to their dogs to get them to hunt particular bits of cover when the going is thick, but this help should not be overdone because some Judges take strong exception to too much interference by the handler. A spaniel should not 'peg' game during its hunting – that is to say, catch and retain or retrieve live unshot game. This gives rise to difficulty, for pheasants can jam themselves in brambles, and rabbits can get stuck too, so that no amount of pushing by the dog will make the game flush. If a dog emerges carrying game and the handler can make it drop it so that it runs or flies away unharmed, the Judge will not downgrade the dog. But if the dog hangs on to the game the Judge must examine it carefully for evidence of injury by shot or the dog. If the latter, the dog is eliminated; but if there is evidence of injury by shot the dog is allowed to run on.

Trials for retrievers are often run in roots which are walked up. Many triallers think that this method tests steadiness to heel very well, and since most of the birds are shot going forward the dogs are tested in marking ability. This method does leave itself open to the oft-quoted charge of artificiality because on a shooting day dogs could not be sent forward to retrieve over unshot ground during which game lying close is almost certain to be disturbed. A trial on a day of driven pheasants is many people's idea of ideal trial conditions. Dogs are tested for steadiness whilst the drive goes on, and this can last a long time with dead birds and runners falling constantly around the dogs. This, say the protagonists, gives dogs a great chance to run-in and to whine and bark and generally show the indiscipline which a first class gundog should not show.

But, this debate apart, you will see from point 14 of the 'Guide to Field Trial Judges' that good gamefinding ability and good fast retrieving is what the trial sets out to test, and this can be proved on birds down in any sort of shooting.

Your dog needs time to graduate to top field trial conditions, and this it can do through Puppy and Novice Stakes where, as point 20 of the 'Guide' explains, 'more leniency is allowed'. A puppy will not be asked to retrieve fur, and a gun will not shoot whilst the puppy is retrieving. Field Trial societies usually suggest in their schedules for Non-Winner and Puppy Stakes that dogs should have some experience of retrieving game in the shooting field before being entered for a trial, and this is a wise precaution because a dog which has done well on dummies, perhaps even in working tests, will not necessarily know how to perform on freshly shot game.

There is much luck in trials, and this cannot be avoided. All retrieves are not of equal difficulty, and whereas one dog may sail through a day getting a series of good, dead, easily marked birds, another may, on its first retrieve, be up against a difficult runner, bad scent, a difficult fall, ground game on the run or many another hazard. The first lucky dog must get a lot of A ratings for its work, whilst the unfortunate second dog will be marked down for failing to overcome horrible problems. Field trial people learn to take this uneven distribution of fortune in their stride, but there is an objectionable type of competitor who grumbles or blames the Judges for his misfortune. He should stay away, for field trials, although involving the serious business of categorising the work of dogs on which many hours of training have been lavished, are essentially amusing and full of good fellowship and commiseration for misfortune.

As a handler at a field trial you will be tense, and this can communicate itself to the dog; but you should try to keep a clear head. Keep your dog on the lead when it is not in the line and let it get the feel of the occasion and the ground so that entry into the line is not too big a change. Try to assess the sort of country into which the birds will fall and be absolutely certain of the wind direction. You can help your dog enormously by getting it down wind of the fall of the bird, for if it goes out on the up-wind side it may miss the bird altogether. Remember that the 'Guide to Field Trial Judges' says, 'A good gamefinding dog should not rely on the handler to find the bird', and 'Dogs showing gamefinding ability and initiative should be placed above those which have to be handled on to their game.' If you can get your dog in a good position relative to the bird's fall, leave it to hunt and find on its own; and if it goes fast and comes back straight you will score well. This does not mean that the whistle should never touch your lips. The dog may have to be handled across difficult country and cover to get to the fall, and whistle and hand signals will be needed to achieve this. Noisy handling is penalised, but adequate handling to direct a dog and correct its line is permissible and necessary.

In a three Judge stake your dog must be seen by two Judges at least before it is discarded unless it is eliminated for one of the 'Eliminating Faults' which are hard mouth, whining or barking, running-in and chasing, out of control, failing to enter water, and deliberately catching unwounded game. So far as hard mouth is concerned all Judges must inspect the crushed bird, and the handler may inspect it too in the presence of the Judges.

You must keep alert when competing at a trial, for if there is a lot of game to recover dogs are taken in and out of the line very rapidly and you need to keep your eye on the steward. Remember that you may carry nothing in your hand, so you must leave your shooting stick with a third person as you go forward. On arrival at the Judge you will be told where to stand, will hand your big number, to be held aloft so that spectators can see when your dog is running, to a steward, remove the dog's lead and put it in your pocket out of sight. Do not send your dog until the judge tells you to and remember that you may move to a more advantageous position if the geography permits; but you will be pulled back if you creep forward too far.

You should keep a supply of water and biscuits in the car, for the dog may well get thirsty, and as he will also be working hard a bit of extra food will do no harm. During long breaks give your dog a place to rest and when it is very wet and cold have a chamois leather cloth available to rub the dog down: a little cossetting will do no harm.

It is not easy to get a place in a field trial nowadays as all stakes are heavily oversubscribed, and since preference in the draw is usually given to members of the society promoting the stake it is necessary to join a whole lot of societies in order to have a chance. It is not unusual for there to be seventy or eighty applicants for a twelve dog stake, so you have to make a lot of applications to get one place. When you are lucky you have won a most precious thing, and it is incumbent upon you not to waste it by bringing an unprepared dog or by not being yourself constantly aware of the dog's problems and of the help needed to help it solve them.

When there are four Judges working in pairs a dog is judged immediately as having been seen by two Judges. When the dogs have all been given their first two or three retrieves the Judges will confer and produce a list of AAA or BBB or CCC dogs. They must all be together to judge the dogs which have come through the first rounds and which are being considered for the top placings, and the Judges may in due course hold a run off for the top places. It may be that the first place has already been decided, and the run-off will be to decide second and third.

Trials for pointer-retrievers may be on a grouse moor as for pointers and setters, or in close cover as for spaniels. Such dogs will be judged on quartering and on pointing like pointers, on pushing into cover like spaniels and on retrieving like spaniels and retrievers. These breeds are worked singly at a field trial, not in pairs as with pointers, setters and spaniels because it is felt that one dog and two guns represents the most usual shooting situations. The Kennel Club's 'Guide to Field Trial Judges' sets out the conduct of these trials and if studied carefully will give a pretty full picture of what is expected of a dog during a trial and what conversely will ensure its downgrading or dismissal from a stake.

CHAPTER ELEVEN

Working Tests

Working tests are not controlled by the Kennel Club but by the various gundog societies which stage them. In these tests conditions of a shooting day are not closely simulated. Birds and ground game are represented by dummies, and gunfire by the discharge of blanks from shotguns. Nevertheless steadiness to heel, dropping to shot, steadiness in a walk-up in line, entering thick covert and getting into and out of water can all be tested. The chief virtue of working tests is that they enable trainers to try their dogs in conditions where there are many dogs around and many people on the move, which is something which cannot be arranged in an ordinary training situation. A dog which performs well in its own familiar meadow can be greatly disoriented when faced with a lot of canine and human bustle, and it must have a chance to get used to this strangeness before it goes out on a shooting day.

Competitors with cocker spaniels at a field trial

A Judge watches a competitor take a dummy from a Labrador

Working tests which take place between the shooting dates of February and September are a wonderful opportunity for this exposure. As with field trials the classes of the stakes vary from Puppy and Novice to Open, and the severity of the tests increases with the seniority of the stake. Competition is fierce, stakes over-subscribed and one criticism of these tests is that trainers keep dogs for test purposes only and thus make the winning of tests an end in itself instead of a stepping stone to field trials and the shooting field.

Judging at working tests is done on a points basis, usually 20 points for each of five tests, and prizes are given according to the number of points scored. Typical retriever tests may include a walk-up in line with five or six dogs walking together. Dummy throwers are in position, and the Judge and the gun walk by one dog at a time. At a signal the gun is fired and the dummy thrown. The dogs must stay steady whilst other dogs retrieve, mark the fall

Marking a dummy fall in the training class

of the dummy thrown for them and go out on retrieve smartly. The walk-up can be made more difficult by having more than one dummy thrown, by having a diversionary elasticated rabbit or by having one dummy seen and another unseen. Then there is a variety of retrieves for the other tests, seen and unseen into cover, seen and unseen over a jump, seen and unseen over water. Every dog undertakes the same test, so it is a nice point whether it is better to be first dog down in an unseen or into cover retrieve, or to come later in the test when the path to the dummy is well trodden. There are advantages and disadvantages in both.

Tests for spaniels and pointer-retrievers are also popular. Ground with good cover to test hunting is used, and often caged pigeons and rabbits simulate game; but at the presumed, though not actual, flush a dummy is thrown and shot at to make the retrieve.

Working tests have another virtue apart from that of giving dogs an opportunity to work together. They are staged at Game Fairs and other country shows, sometimes, on big occasions, with stands built to enable the spectator to get a good view.

Appearance at these shows is fiercely fought for, and there is a tremendous sense of competition from dogs and handlers putting on wonderful performances of control whilst under pressure from the event and the sometimes large audience. These tests give the public a chance to see dogs expertly handled and therefore do much to spread knowledge of what a good gundog should do. That is a very worthwhile function even though some of the dogs running may be criticised for being used specially for working tests and never appearing in the shooting field.

CHAPTER TWELVE

Picking Up

To complete a big day of driven birds there need to be four sorts of dogs: those of the keepers, beaters, guns and pickers-up. Keepers' dogs are of a special sort, hard-working, hard-headed and independent. They must be ready to blank in outlying coverts before the main drive takes place, acting as spaniels through the rough, without too much sign of running-in. Then, when the drive starts, they are in the line with the beaters, pushing birds out of odd corners where they sit tight as the sticks tap past. It is these dogs that cause much of the shouting that echoes through the drive as, getting too far ahead, they push up birds in an unnecessary bouquet.

The keeper's dog is not usually admired, except by the keeper who forgives its peccadilloes for the good things it does, and especially for the dirty work which other dogs would spurn. This is the dog which is at work before the guns are in place, and it probably ends the drive by getting the runner that the smarter dogs have failed on. In any event the keeper's dog will be out the day after the shoot to pick up birds not found the preceding day. He may be joined there by a beater's dog or two, for beaters are often keen and love to work their dogs on retrieves at every opportunity. This chance is denied them on the day as they thrash through the undergrowth keeping birds on the move, unless there is a dogless walking gun, who kills a bird breaking back. Then a beater's dog may get a chance of a retrieve. Beaters' dogs are a necessary evil; they are rarely steady.

The dogs accompanying the guns will be of a special sort, too: not tough enough to do the hard work of the keeper's dog and not steady enough to be worthy of a field trial – an in-between sort of dog. One wonders at its presence at all, for it will almost invariably be tethered during a drive, and almost certainly will be used to pick up birds which could just as easily be picked by hand. There is a good case to be made for banning the gun's dog. Sent for a runner it will balk at hedges or streams, but hunt the foreground purposelessly. Having held up proceedings failing to do its job, the gun's dog is on the trailer to the next drive, covering the guns with mud and making life uncomfortable.

But the picker-up's dogs should be a form of perfection, which, of course, they all too frequently are not. This perfection, be it noted, is nothing to do with field trial expertise, for such expertise is hardly wanted on a shooting day. An exhibition of remote control, by whistle and hand signal, is not at all appreciated, and picking-up is too serious an affair to be entrusted to a future field trial champion at play. Not that many dogs, intended to become field trial champions, will be found picking-up. I recently saw a report of the triumph of a dog in a field trial, and the secretary of the gundog club, reporting the event, thought it worthy of mention that the winner had been picking up only two weeks before the trial. It is a sad, but true, fact that the worst training for a field trial champion is picking-up – just the job it should be most suited to. Why should this be so? It is because the job of picking-up is an unglamorous hard-pounding business, which would destroy a potential field trial champion, destined as it is to be attached to its handler by a thread of control and understanding never to be broken.

The picker-up is not required for most of the picking-up, which is of birds lying within sight of the guns, and should be nowhere near that operation while it is going on. This is the time when the guns' dogs are rocketing around, stumbling upon any and every bird, and dragging them back to their master, whether shot by him or not. When the guns must move on, the picker-up may approach to see if they think there are still birds to find, and, when alone, he must seek them. Here is no opportunity for remote control; the dogs must be left to hunt methodically, criss-crossing the area of fall with no help from the handler, except to call them off and put them into another piece of covert. When possible the handler will stay close to this dogs, and only if there are obstacles to be crossed will he handle them out and away; but mostly he will cross the obstacle himself and follow the dogs' course, taking care not to foul the ground by tramping over it. Having found the missing birds, the picker-up should move on to the next drive, reporting on the way his success or failure, so that the keeper will know whether to come looking the next day.

That is one duty of the picker-up, but his most important job dictates where he should station himself during a drive. The picker-up's main task is to find those birds which fly on after the shot and drop suddenly or plane down, wounded, out of sight of the guns, and for this purpose he must get well back behind the line. Therefore a picker-up should never stand next to a gun, though they too often do. A dogless gun is not an invitation to a picker-up to stand along-

A picker-up well loaded with the product of his dogs' labours

side. This selection of position is important and should be made after consultation with the host or keeper as to whether birds falling behind the guns may be picked or whether they will fall in unshot covert needed for a future drive and to be left undisturbed until then. Having checked this, the picker-up should get back out of sight and out of range of the guns.

As the birds fall they must be marked. This is easily done on a dry day with pencil and paper, by making a small panorama showing prominent features such as trees, streams and gates, and noting the birds down. In bad weather a rough map, drawn on the ground with a stick, will serve the same purpose. Pickers-up need a stick, and one with a crook, for holding back branches and pulling themselves up slopes and to stick in the ground to mark the whereabouts of piled game which, if not marked, may be mislaid.

When the drive is over, and not a second before, the picker-up moves into action by sending a dog for the strongest runner. If at all possible the dog should be taken to where the bird fell and sent off from there. If that dog fails, then a second dog should be tried. A picker-up should be armed with more than one dog – an old and trusted servant and one or two more energetic ones being ideal. Even the energetic ones should be slow workers, using their noses to puzzle out the line, rather than their legs to hunt far and wide. Here is the difference between today's field trial dogs and the ideal picker-up's dog. Field trial Judges go for thrust and style and speed, and today's handlers have produced this to such an extent that the old virtue of steady quartering, leaving no piece of cover uninvestigated, is being bred out of retrievers; and 'hot dogs', too fast for their noses and capable of being handled only by their extremely professional handlers, are taking over. The reason one sees so few steady dogs is that dogs from these strains are too specialist and forceful for the average shooting man to handle.

The picker-up, armed, one hopes, with more suitable material, should bring to hand all the birds he has marked down, and then ask the guns if they have unpicked game. He should never be tempted to put his dogs into covert already being hunted, but should stand aside until the field is clear. The picker-up will have worked well if he returns, adds his game to the game-cart and takes up position for the next drive with no one noticing his presence.

Index

Acknowledgments

The Publishers would like to thank the following for kindly supplying the illustrations on these pages:
John Marchington 31, 49, 52, 53, 59, 68, 96, 142, 144, 154, 201; John Tarleton 21, 51, 60, 67, 112, 119, 167, 191, 196; H. J. L. Osbourn 101 below, 106, 107, 113, 121, 134, 197; Anne Roslin-Williams 25, 26, 27, 28, 33, 37, 38, 55, 56, 57, 58, 69, 72, 75, 76, 82, 83, 85, 86, 87, 88, 89, 98, 100, 101 top two, 102, 103, 104, 105, 109, 110, 111, 114, 115, 120, 123, 126, 128, 129, 132, 152, 158, 159, 162, 164, 195.